Praise for Ac. _____

"'Every time my lithe, dark-haired lover jumped out of her old Toyota truck in baggy boy's cargo shorts and came running up to the door I felt a surge of delight,' writes Elizabeth Bernays, a retired university professor and entomologist. 'This was the woman I had so strangely fallen for.' And 'strangely fallen' she has. Whether she's describing her witty yet uneducated lover's unusual talent for deliberate malapropisms or a first date collecting caterpillars for a research project or their diverse family histories from west Texas to Australia, her passion rises off the page. This heartfelt memoir, full of humor and insight, depicts a life charged with uncertainties and bravery and joy, a life showing us what it's like to take risks to love someone who couldn't be more different from ourselves, and revealing at the same time how utterly unique and yet universal it is to connect emotionally with another human being. *Across the Divide* is an engaging and transformative read."

—Ken Lamberton, author of
Wilderness and Razor Wire and *Chasing Arizona*

"This is a beguiling new memoir by entomologist and writer Elizabeth Bernays. In *Across the Divide*, Bernays tells the story of her love affair with Linda, an unlikely partner in every way. But this book isn't just about the attraction of opposites. It's a rumination on 'seeing'—learning to see nature through each other's eyes and observing oneself changed by the confounding nature of the 'other.'"

—Gail Browne, former director
of the University of Arizona Poetry Center

"Elizabeth Bernays has written a wonderful ode to life's transitions. In the shadow of the loss of her beloved husband and scientific collaborator, she meets Linda, who might as well be from a different planet. Linda helps light a new path for Liz that leads her out of the darkness. Bernays' portrait of her new life as a lesbian and writer is a deeply engaging memoir on the mystery of love, both for people and biodiversity."

—Professor Noah Whiteman,
University of California Berkeley

"Throughout her illustrious entomological career, Liz has delighted in challenging conventional wisdom, proposing and testing novel hypotheses that have profoundly changed the way we think about insects—so it shouldn't come as a surprise that in this later chapter of life, she has again stepped outside the status quo. We are privileged to follow along as Liz turns her famous observational eye inward as well as outward to paint a portrait of a life full of insights, surprises, and love."

—Martha Weiss,
Professor, Georgetown University

Across the
DIVIDE

Other Works by Elizabeth Bernays

Literary books

House of Pictures 2009

Three Miles: A Walk for all Seasons 2011

Six Legs Walking: Notes from an Entomological Life 2019

Children's books with Linda Hitchcock (Gheen)

Saving Pocket 2007

The Pocket Book 2008

Just Pocket 2009

Entomology book with R. F. Chapman

Host-plant Selection by Phytophagous Insects 1994

Across the
DIVIDE

The Strangest Love Affair

ELIZABETH BERNAYS

Across the Divide: The Strangest Love Affair

Published by Wheatmark®
2030 East Speedway Boulevard, Suite 106
Tucson, Arizona 85719 USA
www.wheatmark.com

ISBN: 979-8-88747-087-0 (paperback)
ISBN: 979-8-88747-041-2 (ebook)
LCCN: 2023901141

Previously published stories by Elizabeth Bernays that are included in the following chapters:
1. "First Date with Hairy Caterpillars," *Umbrella Factory,* September 31, 2020
2. "Back in the Desert," *Shooter Literary Magazine*, November 17, 2020
3. "Road Trip," *Adelaide Magazine*, November 18, 2020
4. "Discovering," *Toasted Cheese*, August 23, 2021
5. "Linda in the Desert," *The Fourth River*, April 19, 2022

Bulk ordering discounts are available through Wheatmark, Inc. For more information, email orders@wheatmark.com or call 1-888-934-0888.

Contents

Acknowledgments

FIRST, I WANT TO thank my wife, Linda Hitchcock, who is the heroine in this story. She taught me about new worlds and provided endless entertainment, but I am particularly grateful for her patience as I labored on this book. Annie Rosenthal got me started on this project and the people in my writer group provided important criticism and feedback, especially Ken Lamberton, who made me delve more into meanings and always had excellent ideas for improvement. Gillian Haines, Michele Rappoport, and Dora Rollins had many good ideas for making the writing better. And I have benefited from critiques of individual chapters by innumerable friends and relatives.

1 First Date with Hairy Caterpillars

BLACK, HAIRY CATERPILLARS WERE warming themselves in the early-morning sun on the tops of bushes. Later they would crawl briskly on the ground, searching for their favorite small food plants to eat. They would be more difficult to catch then. This was the hour.

"Look here, bub," I called, "a whole lot of them. We might get all we need in one place!"

I had only known Linda for a couple of months and was finishing research on a caterpillar project before ending my entomological career. I invited her to come with me to collect woolly bear caterpillars in the field—something we could do together. She was reluctant *and* intrigued but came to my place for the night, and we set off early the next morning to Gardner Canyon, fifty miles south of Tucson. We tramped into the hackberry and desert honeysuckle bushes with a backpack full of vials.

Linda pushed through the bushes. Her loud voice rang out. "They's what you wanna get a hundred of? They's big-ass bugs. Jeez, do I need to touch the suckers? Look at this one crapping on hisself." She looked at me with worried eyes. "Can't do it, babe."

I took a few vials out of my pack, removed a cork from

one of them, and gently edged a caterpillar into the vial with one finger. Replacing the cork, I held it up to look at.

"See? Easy."

As Linda gingerly collected specimens, she said, "It's real naarce out here, hey, and I's a scientist too now."

I was getting used to the strident voice with a strong nasal accent, single syllables becoming two, new words and phrases.

"Fuck, these grasses itching my laygs." Then she was off: "Where I live at the resort, I's been doing stain glass, me and Bobbi joking all the time. You shoulda seen this guy pretending to have dementia, and a lady kept saying, 'Sad, ain't it?'"

We worked in silence for a while, and then she said, "I think religious politicians should be shutted up."

My mother in Australia would have been appalled by Linda's speech. She was never gifted in the humor department, but I found Linda smart and funny.

From time to time, I heard a loud "sonsofbitches!" or "fuck!" as Linda searched. She had encountered a spiny plant, an unexpected grasshopper, a spider, or a stick vaguely resembling a snake. For me, the work was automatic. How often had I collected insects of one sort or another! Australian plague locusts caught in a net that flew behind a Land Rover as my partner, Reg, and I drove the outback and discussed the population size; wandering in Saharan Mali, searching for the grasshoppers seen with radar the night before, Reg in cloth hat poking sticks down likely cracks in ground that had been mud in a long-ago rain. As I searched the vegetation for caterpillars this fine summer morning in a southern Arizona wash, all my past entomological life with the loved partner who had died too soon ran through my mind, while I wondered at this new adventure with such a different mate.

A bunch of caterpillars was already on the ground, running around from plant to plant.

"Jeez, babe, they's haulin' ass!"

An hour or so produced just seventeen caterpillars, so we clattered on over the rough road to the west side of the Santa Rita Mountains and down Box Canyon, stopping at several sites on the way to just look around. I always liked to explore the canyons and see what might be new and interesting. Near the pass to Box Canyon, I glimpsed a plant with white flowers. I wondered, *Is that a horsetail milkweed?* I hadn't seen it here before, so we got out of the car, and I climbed down into the dry wash, leaving Linda at the top. I had hardly reached the bottom when I heard an alarmed voice:

"Biz!"

"What do you mean?" I called up.

"Biz, biz, biz . . . listen."

I remained still, trying to figure out what she meant, and suddenly recognized the buzz of honeybees. Linda was so severely allergic to them that she sometimes wore a bracelet with first-aid information. I rushed up to the car where she stood immobile. I was sure the bees were interested only in the flowers of the Arizona rosewood tree above her, but for now I had to forget the damned milkweed. As I got back in the car with Linda, I thought, *Biz equals bees. Must remember that.* She had, in fact, been bitten by something small, and she kept looking at the spot as we waited for symptoms that never came.

We drove on to Lower Box Canyon. There we picked up a lot of caterpillars that were already feeding, mostly on thread-leaf groundsel. I noticed several favorite food plants of the caterpillars, including Arizona popcorn flower, which contains toxic chemicals that these caterpillars eat with great enthusiasm. Between meals, they literally ran along the ground.

"Jeez, they's tons over here!"

"Yes, they really gallop. Can you catch some?"

"I guess. Them suckers are fast."

A little later, "Sonsofbitches, do you work out here all day?"

Linda's interest in caterpillars began to flag, or perhaps she was getting tired in the heat.

Nearby was a big Emory oak, where we sat in the shade.

"Break time," I called, fishing sandwiches out of my pack.

"What's that crap?"

"Havarti cheese and spinach on multigrain."

"Oh Gawd, foo-foo food—not for me."

I smiled. It would be some time before I learned all her tastes in food. She liked Wonder Bread, hamburger (well cooked), and fries. Her absolute favorite was boiled lobster with butter. Most sweet foods were good: rice-crispy bars ("crispy critters"), brownies, and red velvet cake were favorites. The first time I made dinner at home for Linda and two friends, she decided the chicken marsala was not for her, and she foraged for herself in the kitchen, where she "fixed good shit": a tin of tuna, mayonnaise, and crustless white bread.

We were silent for a while as a Mexican jay scrabbled noisily in another oak up the hill. But Linda was not the quiet type. As I ate, I heard about a childhood in Texas and photography with the fire department in Dallas. I lay back in the grass and watched small puffy white clouds rushing past the leaves above. They took me back to a childhood in Australia—summer days spent lying alone under the jacaranda tree in a back garden with the same little white puffs against the same deep blue. And my mind wandered to the days of chasing dreamy blue Melissa butterflies and watching caterpillars chewing leaves in my mother's garden. It was there, when I was ten, that I first became fascinated with insects.

Linda squatted awkwardly on the ground, watching me.

Why was she so quiet, I wondered. Eventually, hunger got the better of her.

"You's woofing that bread; give me a bit of the crap, babe."

She ate warily, spitting out the larger grains, but then suddenly burst into a fit of coughing. I did the usual things—bang on the back, water to drink—but it took some minutes before she could answer the question "Gone down the wrong way?"

"Fuck, that's what happens—bits get stuck at the back on my hangy-down guy."

We lay back again in the long grass.

"This woolly bear we've been getting is amazing, you know. The caterpillars eat these poisonous plants and absorb the chemical in it for themselves so that predators won't eat them."

"Cool."

"Yes, and it's even better than that. Once they become moths and mate, the dad gives his toxic stuff to the mom so she can put it into her eggs and protect them too."

"Uh-huh."

I pulled out my last card. "And guess what—the same chemicals are used by the male to make a scent that excites the females to have sex with him."

"You work on that? Jeez! I did tell Bobbi I was going out to get caterpillars with you and do field crap, but are you going to study sex or what? Do they have little dickies?"

"Well, the sex story is more or less worked out, and there is a guy in North Carolina who is concentrating on that. I'll send him and his students some eggs when we get the next lot in the lab."

We rested in silence while I gazed at the grasses bending with the light breeze, admiring delicate flowers hanging from such tender stems. My mind went to why the grasses around us here in Lower Box Canyon were different from those in Gardner Canyon. Was it soil, elevation, rainfall, or some complicated interaction with other plants and animals? Perhaps it had to do with the slopes facing east or west. Perhaps Lehman's love grass had been introduced and now had a foothold on one side of the mountains, whereas on the other, with gramma grasses and bush Muhly grass, the invasion had yet to occur.

As the temperature rose, my thoughts faded.

Linda started picking at tiny seeds on her sneakers. "What you gonna do with these guys?"

"You'll see if you come up to my lab in a couple of days."

"Oh, you clever little Sarcophilous." She'd never met anyone with such a weird interest in insects.

As I stared into the distance, imagining my experiments, Linda rubbed a red spot on her arm with concern. She flicked small flies from her face and started on her third bottle of water. She'd already warned me that she had ADHD, and I decided to leave it at that for the time being. Just the day before, after I'd tried to explain my experiments on grasshoppers, Linda said, "Okay, good, you just get on with your shit while I watch *The Ellen DeGeneres Show*." That was fine by me; I was able to concentrate if she had something else to do. She called all my work *shit*, whether it was science or reading for writing classes or working on an essay, and I quickly realized it was not a pejorative but in some sense an affectionate expression of my interest in all the things she didn't share. Apparently, lots of nice things were "shit" anyway. Good shit.

Linda was surprised and flattered to be invited out into the field, and it had been an adventure, certainly a novelty, and an eye-opener about her lover—my passion for the study of plants and insects, my curiosity about how things worked in the biological world, my obsession with getting what I needed for experiments. But Linda was pleased to get home without encountering snakes or any biting insects. She did complain of scratches and inexplicable red dots on her skin and felt sure she had worse allergy problems, but she was a great storyteller. Now she had a whole lot of ammunition for new tales. She would certainly exaggerate about me, the doctor (but not a real one). I imagined, "You shoulda seen Liz climbing miles down a canyon to look for a single black hairy guy and not even looking for snakes." She would certainly embroider our field adventures when she talked to her neighbors, people whose lives were consumed with casinos, spas, and tidy living in a retirement resort where everyone was much older than she was.

I took the caterpillars we collected back to the laboratory and put each in a small cup with a block of synthetic diet. Two days later, Linda came to see the next stage of the work and how the caterpillars' taste buds responded with incredible sensitivity (one in a trillion parts in water) to a group of chemicals called alkaloids—the toxins they get from plants for their own defense against predators and parasites. The new experiment was an extension of what I had found earlier that the alkaloids the caterpillars ate protected them from parasitic flies. Could it also be that caterpillars with parasites in them had greater sensitivity to the alkaloids, making them feed even more on alkaloid-containing plants? That way, the caterpillar could self-medicate with more of the toxin when it was parasitized. It was a somewhat wild idea, but that is where biology is such fun. Wild ideas sometimes turn out to be true.

Linda watched as I prepared caterpillars for testing their taste buds. Each inch-long larva was held in a small water-filled vial with a rubber halter around the neck and head sticking out above.

"See, bub, water stops air from getting into the breathing holes down the sides of their bodies, and they get anesthetized."

"Cool."

When the wriggling stopped, I trimmed the hairs round the taste buds with tiny scissors. I set the vial in a clamp, with all the fine recording wires ready. Specially machined manipulators reduced my hand's actions to minute movements so the testing solutions could be brought carefully to the taste bud.

"Babe," Linda insisted, "it's too small."

"You can look at it. Let's get the eyepieces in the right place for your eyes."

"Sonsofbitches, there's no way of seeing stuff."

"It's only a matter of magnification." I adjusted the focus. "Take a look down here."

"Fuck!"

"The little spikes of electric currents from the taste cell, which tell you about sensitivity, are small. They must be magnified, cleaned up, and looked at later with a computer. One hundred spikes per second is a big response; five spikes per second is almost nothing."

"Yeah, babe, sure."

"Well, you wanted to know."

"I's had it for now; it's not like *Animal Planet*."

We laughed as she made fun of my ignorance about TV and my knowledge and enthusiasm about science.

I tested every insect we'd collected to record how sensitive each individual was to the favorite toxic chemical. Would the ones more sensitive to the chemical be the ones that contained parasites?

"What's next?" Linda said at the end of that first day.

"It will take a few weeks," I said, leaving her to wonder. But she tuned out quickly and regaled me with tales of TV stars SpongeBob SquarePants and Siegfried and Roy. Eventually, she realized my mind was somewhere else.

"Hey, do you actually know any a' these shows?"

I had to admit I had no idea what they were.

"What? Not hearda them? Ever heard of *Vegas*? Eh, Doctor?" She loved to tell people she met, and people at her resort, how little I knew, how I don't watch television. "She don't even know who Siegfried and Roy are, for fucksake. She's an opera buff, a symphony nut." For my part, I was quite happy to be this way, and her joking was, at some level, a measure of her interest in me. Linda is still figuring out my strange lifestyle with minimal stuff and old-fashioned housewares, never mind the total lack of interest in shopping. She knows I don't want to buy anything, change anything, or enter the consumer world. Still, she did get me to buy a clock with luminous numbers, a radio, nightlights, a coffeemaker, pruning clippers, lights for the porch, new tires, and even a new laptop computer.

Back in the lab, I removed each caterpillar from its watery vial, dried its hairy body with a tissue, and placed it on a warm plate to recover "consciousness." After they were put back in their little numbered cups to feed, I put them aside to see which ones later gave rise to the adult moths and which just gave rise to parasites. Individuals that housed fly parasites wouldn't make it to the adult, moth stage. Before the caterpillar could even think about getting ready for the transformation, the flies completed their maggot lives inside and burrowed out of the caterpillar, leaving nothing but a shrunken cuticle or skin.

A lot of the time, I worked alone. Linda didn't have the

interest to persevere with anything long-winded. I wondered about her tastes in food and how her taste buds might be different from mine. Did she have a special sensitivity to her beloved lobster flavor? Lobster tastes like nothing to me.

I already knew that the special taste cell in the caterpillars that responded so sensitively to the alkaloid could shut down altogether if the caterpillar fed for too long on a plant containing high levels. This was good because too much of the chemical can reduce growth. So this insect with such a tiny brain had the capacity to regulate the amount of alkaloid it consumed by reducing the sensitivity of its taste buds.

The new study was to see if it could also become more sensitive if it needed to protect itself from parasites.

On my computer, I compared the results of my recordings from taste buds and my data on the parasite history of the caterpillars to see if there could be a relationship between taste sensitivity and parasitism. It was one of those moments of excitement at possibilities, and I was almost shaking with anticipation and impatience. Do the parasites make a difference to sensitivity of the taste buds? If they did, it would be such a novelty. Linda doesn't share my enthusiasm for this idea. She looks at me with amazement when I wax passionate about some biological observation, but she also likes me this way. It's as if she has her own protégé who has developed a crazy interest; as if she's a guide, pleased that her pupil is engaged in something that excites her.

As I collated the data, I gradually began to see a pattern, but I didn't dare to believe there was one until I compiled all the numbers and did the statistics. Then, joy! Caterpillars that had taste buds much more responsive to the alkaloids were the ones that housed parasites. This would make them feed more on plants containing the chemicals like that Arizona popcorn plant I had noted on our field trip. They would gorge on alkaloid-containing plants and in this way kill some of the parasites within. It was self-medication! Such a change in taste receptors is not known in other animals and remains a rather novel idea.

Linda looked at me. She was fascinated, not by the findings but by my excitement. "Jeez, you really get into this shit, don't you?"

"I love it."

"You so passionate, you little professor, you sincopsy."

I smiled at her made-up word.

My research is a small contribution to knowledge, but for me it is the total exhilaration of being a scientist—finding something new and unexpected. I am also fascinated by Linda and in trying to understand her and what makes her tick. It is another kind of study.

After I told Linda about the published paper, she felt part of the enterprise in some way, but she had no real comment except to say, "I love you. You so animated."

And I laughed. "I love you too, you little raccoon."

New caterpillar questions kept percolating in my head, but I didn't bother to tell her. My former students continued the research and published their results. Linda was just happy and proud to be associated with me and my work, and she had her own, different kind of knowledge to share with me. She had a much quicker grasp than I ever had of much of today's technology and celebrities, TV channels and cars and cell phones, so she enjoyed explaining or helping. And always, she loved to make me laugh with crazy jokes that help me to forget the dark side of life.

It also interested me greatly that Linda immediately seized the meaning of my wilder writings when my colleagues tended to be perplexed by them. I showed her something I produced when Reg was sick. The last section goes:

there is my arm sweeping with the solar wind
there is my hair a shooting star
my aorta is Iguassu Falls
my vein is the Amazon
there is my leg jumping over India
there is my foot manacled to a wreck at the dump

"Yeah, that's you doing your work that you loved all around the world, but Reg sick, so you stayed home."
I turned to her with a silent hug.

2 The Beginning: Finding Linda

IN THE SMALL, SHABBY living room of an old house in downtown Tucson, Arizona, a dozen women sat waiting. It was 2004 at a lesbian support group run by Wingspan—a center for the LGBTQ+ community. The large facilitator came in, plonked down on a dilapidated armchair, and passed around a sheet of paper for names and email addresses.

It was a motley gathering, and each woman had a different concern.

"How'm I going to tell my husband?"

"What'll happen to my children?"

"It's so lonely. I got no friends."

Most extraordinary was the small, swarthy woman with a strong London accent, who ranted and raved about a guy trying to kill her.

There were other stories of loss and despair. Several expressed hatred of men. After having had a wonderful husband and still mourning his death, I found them annoying but wondered what dreadful experiences had caused such powerful aversion.

Across from me, a darkly tanned woman in shorts cried uncontrollably, but she finally managed to explain. "I's married to a man who knows I's gay, but my lover just dumped me."

This was Linda. Did her husband really tolerate a wife who had affairs with women?

There was no way I could tell the story of how close Reg and I had been, how perfectly woven together our passions for research, classical music, and theater were. Our marriage had been one of true soulmates, and we worked together on agricultural problems in different countries around the world. I spoke quietly about misery since the death of an adored husband and the emergence of an intense physical attraction to women.

After seeing me in subdued clothes with hands awkwardly clutched, Linda told me afterward that she thought I was a timid British housewife type. At the end of the session, I took note of the three email addresses of women who had mentioned the complication of a man in their lives. Perhaps we would have something in common. It was only Linda who replied. "See ya next time."

As the same old stories were recounted at the next group meeting, I looked across the room at Linda, and our eyes met. I felt a mutual recognition that the evening would be tedious, but a connection had been established between us, and at the end of the session, we left together.

Linda turned to me. "Did ya hear that girl who's been going for six years? Fuck, that's not for me."

I looked at her. I was fascinated by this woman with unfamiliar mannerisms and speech. "If people need it for so long, it can't be all that useful. Let's not go back."

Walking in silence, I desperately wondered how to prolong our time together. "Want to get a drink?"

"I guess."

Not much enthusiasm, it seemed! It turned out Linda

didn't drink wine or beer; didn't want tea, coffee, juice, or soda. I was puzzled, but in a small café, we sat at bare wooden tables and drank plain water. I thought, *This is weird—I got her in here, but what the hell do we talk about?*

We sat quietly, and the minutes got longer. So I began: "Where are you from?"

"Dallas. And you? From England?"

"Oh, well, I'm Australian but lived in England for twenty years. Been in the States since '83—hybrid."

We looked each other over. We were of similar height, but that was where the similarity ended. Linda's fine brown skin, bright dark eyes, and black hair in a buzz cut made her look younger than her forty-nine years. Her build was boyish, with no waist. By contrast, I had wavy graying hair, fair skin, and a distinctly curvy figure. At sixty-two, I also looked somewhat younger.

Linda gulped down her water. "What'a you do for a living?"

"Retired from teaching. And you?"

Linda looked away and, after a long pause, replied, "Freelance photojournalist. Where'd ya teach?"

"I was at the University of Arizona."

"Jeez, you a professor or somethin'?"

"Yes."

"I never met a professor."

I took a sip of water, wishing it was something alcoholic as I desperately tried to think of what else to say. During the long minutes, her face grew serious, and I felt the evident ache she suffered. Because of my own sadness, I felt closer to her. The short hair made her seem vulnerable. I decided that she was very appealing.

Eventually, Linda leaned over. "I dropped outta school in eighth grade, but you went to college!"

"Yes, I went to university in Australia and also in England."

"Well!"

I laughed and decided to tell her more. "I studied insects and got a PhD in entomology."

"I thought you never been anywhere, the way you sat there all prim and proper." She smiled, and her little face lit up, so her dark eyes seemed even brighter. This sassy woman was unlike anyone I had ever met. "What else?"

I took in her Texan accent as she proceeded. "I dropped out, like I said, and didn't want to work a regular job. I was stoned outta my mind for years and years."

Everything we each said made it plain that no two women could have backgrounds more different. I had had what my mother called a "proper" upbringing in Australia and later, after a year drinking in every pub in London, became a scientist and then a professor. But I was intrigued by a new side of life. Linda seemed doubtful about someone from a world she couldn't even imagine. Later, she told me that she did think to herself, *At least she don't seem uppidee.*

We left the café and wandered to our parked cars. She turned to face me before opening the car door, and I felt a sudden rush of attraction. We were silent for moment, looking into each other's eyes. Never had such a fascination riveted my senses. Impulsively, "I love you" burst out of me.

"Oh no, you don't." She jumped into her truck.

I was excited by the very idea of a relationship with someone so different from everything and everybody I had ever known. It satisfied another part of me—I had always bucked convention. It was such a new feeling to be freely attracted to a woman after a relationship with a man I had loved for so long. Reg and I shared everything, and our communications often required no words, even as he lay dying in our desert home. After eighteen months of loss and desperation, I had discovered Wingspan.

My beloved mother had been dead for decades, and her preferences were no longer relevant, but she would have been appalled by Linda's English and even more so by her Texas accent and lack of education. When my older brother Barton became engaged to a girl whose drunken, uneducated family was living in rundown government housing, they were considered "the bottom of the barrel." She was beside herself. I wondered what my other relatives would think of Linda. I knew many academic colleagues would find my attraction to Linda mysterious. What happened to being an intellectual? What on earth would we have in common? My feeling of defiance was satisfying. Even in my childhood years in school, I had reveled in the forbidden and loved small-scale jokes, like coming into class late, dragging six strings behind me, and saying to the teacher, "Sorry I'm late, Miss Gray. Schultz had pups." But she was the teacher who enjoyed jokes: "Alright, Elizabeth, just tie them up at my front desk." I would never be given responsibilities because I was the naughtiest girl in the school, and I enjoyed that title. I never told my mother.

Linda and I emailed each other, and a week or so later, she agreed to visit me at my ranch house in the Tucson foothills. We ambled around in the pristine Sonoran Desert looking at cottontail rabbits, lizards, and quail. "Look at that tarny bunny and that big o' fat lizard; he's a football!" Linda was fearful of snakes, and when she saw a stick: "Wot's that thang? Whoa, looks like a snake." Despite the possible dangers, she seemed to enjoy our walk and my sharing occasional bits of natural history. Until "I'm wore out," and we went in.

Linda gazed around at the large old ranch house with huge beams, red cement floors, and picture windows looking out to saguaros and prickly pear with the Santa Catalina Mountains beyond. She took in the oil paintings and water-colors on the walls but was most fascinated by a picture of African village life created in bas relief on beaten aluminum.

"What's that?"

"Reg and I bought that when we were working in Nigeria. The artist is Asiru Olatunde, and he worked with just a hammer and nails. We got it for just a few dollars back then, but it's worth thousands now."

"Cool."

She looked around the Arizona room with its metal stove, old TV, and glass sliding doors leading out to a big patio and the desert beyond. Finally, she looked at all the shelves of books.

"You read all these?"

"Mostly."

Then she saw my old Bible among the poetry books.

"You religious?"

"I'm an atheist, but I had a religious phase when I was a teenager."

"Yeah, well, I knew I was an atheist when I got to about ten and just stopped going to the church with my parents."

"What did they say to that?"

"They never said nothin' against what I did."

After a short silence, she smiled. "Well, we got something in common, eh?"

Conversation stalled, and Linda took to organizing the books on one of the shelves so that the titles all went one way. "Gotta have 'em straight."

At last, we both relaxed a bit, and Linda went on in her Texas dialect and drawl. "I guess I like reading. I got a list of a hundred top books from the *New York Times*, bought them second hand at Bookman's. I's reading them one by one."

This unschooled woman was not just smart and funny. There was a lot more to find out about her.

"Would you like tea?" I offered.

"Nah, just water."

"What about some dinner?"

"I gotta go home."

She was sitting on the old leather sofa as I stood in front of her. We looked at one another for several minutes. I saw that round, smiling face with dimpled cheeks and badly wanted to kiss her. Perhaps Linda saw that because she quickly left with scarcely a goodbye.

A couple of weeks later, we agreed to meet at a Wingspan social. Linda mixed with dozens of others, chatting and laughing, but I struck up a conversation with a woman interested in birdwatching, and she recommended a new book about birds in Arizona. I took out my ever-present notebook to write down the title and author. Suddenly, out of nowhere, Linda was there kissing me on the mouth.

I laughed with surprise and pleasure. "Look, she's told me about a great book on birding."

"I was over there talking and thought you was getting her phone number, and Brenda said, 'Watch out! That lady is taking your new friend,' so I come over to get you. Well, nothing but a stupid book."

She looked at the notebook and then at me. We gazed at one another for a time that seemed endless but was probably no more than a few seconds before Linda broke the silence with a loud laugh. I thought, *She is excited now too.*

Later, Linda said Brenda told her that scientists in lab coats were the most exciting for sex. "Not that I care what Brenda thinks, but it is pretty funny—do you wear a lab coat?"

That evening, as I sat looking out at the desert I loved, I

thought about the social. I had met a very diverse group, and what a new experience it had been to meet a lot of lesbians. In the normal course of events in my life, there was no way that Linda and I would ever have met. If we had somehow been brought into contact in a different context, neither of us would have recognized the other as someone to befriend.

Next time, we met on a date. Linda picked me up in her old Toyota truck on a warm, summer Saturday evening, and we drove to the Arizona-Sonora Desert Museum. It is a place and time for great sunsets, stars, night-blooming cereus, and evening primroses. Bats and raccoons were emerging from their daytime sleep. We were exhilarated by a storm over the valley, with dramatic clouds and intermittent thunder and lightning. It presaged an exciting chemistry between us, but I wondered if Linda might be hesitant about being involved with a "professor type."

"Have you been here in the evening before?" I wondered.

"Nah. You?"

"A few times."

We went on in silence. I wondered, *Will I ever get to know this curious Texan?*

I know that Linda wondered, *What the hell am I doing with a fucking professor?*

On the way home, Linda drove into a lonely picnic area surrounded by palo verde trees and cholla cactus plants, where we kissed seriously for the first time. I wanted to linger, but before I could say anything, Linda started the engine and drove back to my place. She left immediately, almost without a goodbye.

It wasn't long before she came to visit again when I proposed dinner. By this time, I knew that Linda had a very limited diet—nothing fancy or spicy or unusual. I served steak, potatoes, and beans.

Linda was at ease and affectionate while making fun of me or others. On the other hand, I needed wine to reduce tension and make talking easier. I felt, though, that we were gradually learning to understand each other. We each had a bath, and we kissed. Then Linda suddenly left me to sleep in the spare room.

The following week, Linda offered to cook. She happily wielded tongs at my old Kettle barbecue grill as I watched her in baggy plaid shorts, T-shirt, and sneakers out on the patio through the sliding glass doors. Those restless boy legs dancing a little jig for a minute added to my pleasure as I drank my wine. She brought in the steak, and I was immediately aware of prominent nipples under her loose T-shirt, though I already knew she never wore a bra. I could have been distracted by imagining more, but Linda had questions.

"When did you leave Australia?" she asked as we ate.

"When I was twenty-two, I left Sydney by ship with my friend Lucy. We disembarked in Gibraltar and hitchhiked all around Europe."

"Then what?"

"Well, we had a bit of a wild time. Then I taught high school, and eventually I did a PhD at the University of London. After that, I was a British government scientist and worked in places like India and Nigeria and Mali."

Linda kept sipping her water. Finally, she put down her glass. "Well, I don't know whatcha want with a dropout who did nothing."

"You were a photojournalist, so that's really interesting."

"I guess. I did sell stuff to the *Dallas Times Herald* and the AP; mostly I worked with the fire department."

I could imagine she was a pro when it came to any photographic work involving quick decisions. Linda was friends with the local fire chief in Lewisville, Texas, and had begun taking photographs of fires and anything involving responses to fires and accidents. She said she enjoyed the adrenaline rush and always got to the scenes fast. I knew she was quick, so it made sense that she would be the one with the best shots.

Linda turned to questions that I had no quick answer for: What do you do for fun? What do you watch on TV? But she didn't really seem to need answers.

She spread out on the sofa, seemingly relaxed.

I said, "Would you like a massage?"

"No."

"Well, then, here I come," and I leaned over to kiss her.

"No, you don't," she said, jumping up. "You pounced on me."

On other occasions, she left quite suddenly and without explanation. Much later, Linda confessed she had sometimes left because she was nervous about me and nervous about anything physical. Alone, I was left wondering. What made this woman tick? What kind of relationship does she have with her husband, John? Is she interested in me really?

One summer day, she suggested I join her and John at a bowling alley and I would meet him. It turned out that the date, August 13, was their wedding anniversary, so it felt very uncomfortable. Still, nothing was going to stop me from going to see her bowl. I watched them. They had their own balls, and they often made strikes. My eyes were mostly on Linda, so alive and so limber, joking with all the bowlers and observers. Her tall husband, with thin sandy hair and beard, was quietly friendly. As Linda laughed with another bowler, he smiled at me. "Lin always talks to everyone, and she's told me about you."

How was it possible John accepted me, knowing that Linda and I were already attracted to each other? In any case, he apparently became aware of electricity in the air.

"Lin, do you and Liz want to take off?"

That's all it took. The two of us went to my house, and we sat in the Arizona room watching Gambel's quail marching around outside.

"Does John really not mind your having an affair?"

"Oh, he got used to it when I went with Kim. John and me's friends, and we got Trooper. He's a yellow Lab and the best dog we ever had. We got Wookie too. You'd love him. He's a Yorkie and such a character. When it's raining, he can open the doggie door and pee through it without going outside and getting wet. He's got a million tricks."

I thought back to my teenage years when we had Australian terriers that are very like Yorkies, but Linda had moved on from dogs.

We ate dinner on the patio just outside the open sliding glass doors, where a cool, damp breeze from the evaporative cooler bathed us. It was the usual—steak, potato, and beans, while Linda drank water, and I had my favorite red wine. Mexican long-nosed bats flew by and stole sugar water from the hummingbird feeder, and javelina trotted past the patio. A coyote howling in the distance broke into our silence.

Later, I was in bed when she came into the bedroom and announced, "I'm going to make love to you tonight."

I found this amusing. I lay there warm and excited from alcohol and pondered this strange relationship as she showered. It came back to me that there had been a time, perhaps twenty-five years earlier, when I had begun to fall for tall, handsome Sandy, an imposing woman who reminded me of the teacher I had a crush on in high school. And Sandy was inviting. But nothing was going to interfere with my relationship with Reg. He was everything, so I stopped seeing Sandy, and the short lesbian flash faded completely.

I was still musing on the past when a warm, damp Linda jumped in beside me, and we kissed. Slowly, we felt one another's bodies.

"I love you, bub," I whispered as I rubbed my hand over her back.

"I loves you too, babe, so let's see those hooter-monkeys—what a huge aurora borealis."

I laughed. "You're so funny," but neither of us knew if our affair would lead anywhere in the long term.

Linda joked, "Anniversary of our first night gonna be the same date as me and John's wedding anniversary!"

3 Discovering

EVERY TIME MY LITHE, dark-haired lover jumped out of her old Toyota truck in baggy boy's cargo shorts and came running up to the door, I felt a surge of delight. This was the woman I had so strangely fallen for.

"I loves you, babe," she called.

"And I love you, bublet."

After a long hug, we sat together on the sofa in my Arizona room with a view of the mesquite tree full of chirpy house finches. "What's new?" I asked.

"Bobbi and Glen arrived yesterday, and they got the same RV spot they had last year. Charlene asked if I got a new friend."

I took her small hand in mine. "Tell me about your family."

"Okay, well, Mom and Dad worked all day in a shoe shop. Later, Mom did the housework, and after we ate, Dad and I watched TV—just the programs I wanted. I would call out, 'Mom, come and change the channel!' She would reply, 'I'm in the middle of something,' but we called again, and she dropped whatever and fixed the channel for us."

We were quiet as I pictured the spoiled child and the mother servant. "My father was an attorney, but he was so silent I never really knew him."

But Linda's eyes were on Tigger, my tabby cat. "He don't like me. He runs away. Mom and Dad were Methodists and went to church every Sunday. They didn't say much, but they never talked bad about anyone. When I was about ten, my best friend was a Black kid."

My mother believed she was not prejudiced, but she had such expressions as "Tidy up your room; it looks like a Blacks' camp." And no one thought twice about the can of Gollywog-brand marmalade with a caricature of a Black kid on the label. I told Linda we were Church of England, and my parents thought everyone else was inferior. "Those people are Baptists," Mother would say about the family next door. "And pale faces," Father added because the women didn't wear makeup. "The Durants down the road are Roman Catholics—bog Irish, and they work in a *shop!*"

Linda turned to me. "Hey, your eyes are spotted! Gotta shoot a picture of them," and I smiled as our eyes met before she leaned over and kissed each eye.

As I ran my hand through her soft buzz cut, I thought about Mother wanting us to know about the Church—it was part of our class consciousness. And yet she would say that the main thing was the Sermon on the Mount, and nothing else really mattered. But I went to another story. "Everyone was white in our Brisbane suburb. Jackie and I would sit underneath a passion fruit vine on hot summer days and talk through the wire fence. Mrs. Jones would say, 'Yous kids, I gonna have a cuppa tea an' a Bex an' a good lay down.' Mother said that the neighbors were very *ordinary*. That was the worst thing my mother could say about anyone."

Linda stood and whirled her arms. She looked for birds in the mesquite and then said, "Where's that asshole kitty gone?" We walked out among the prickly pear and bursage as I thought of our contrasted but relatively frugal childhoods.

My father hated sending bills, and money was always short, but what money we had was spent on the private education of the four of us children.

Linda continued. "Dad loved animals and always had a dog on his lap, and he always gave me what I wanted—dogs, cats, even a horse, and a ton of other things, and I don't know how he did it. Mom made breakfast bars I liked out of rice and butter and sugar, or I had cake or ice cream. There was always red velvet cake—I love that shit. At dinner, Dad would ask, 'Only Queenie gets the lamb chops?'"

Linda's parents had been accepting of her requests and decisions, especially about not going to school, and my mind turned again to my upbringing, and *you must have a profession, darling!* Mother would have derided Linda's parents, yet I learned to repeat prejudices, while Linda had ideas of her own.

Next time Linda came to my house, we went out on the patio and watched hummingbirds at the feeder—always competing for a place at the sugar water. We stood as a redheaded male Anna's hummingbird pecked at the green broad-billed and chased him off.

"Look at that red guy. What an asshole."

The scene was repeated several times, keeping Linda's attention. But I pushed, "Why did you drop out of school?"

Linda plopped down on a garden chair with a sigh. "What? Oh, I felt different from everyone. I played some games with the boys, but I was often alone. I got bullied in the playground, and you wouldn't believe how many of them took drugs. I got an A in everything—so bored, and I was glad to drop out in eighth grade."

"And your parents didn't care?"

"No. If I didn't want to go to school, I stayed with my parents at the shoe shop where they worked or played with friends who lived near the shop. Sometimes, when Dad drove me to school, and I decided when we got close that I didn't want to go, he would say, 'Well, get down so no one can see you,' and we would drive past.

"Mom believed that punishments, or even rules, for me was wrong. When her best friend said she should be disciplining me, she said, 'If you keep on with that talk, we can't stay friends.'"

Communication took strange turns as I learned her way of speaking. And she shrieked with derision when I used an unfamiliar word: "*Pernicious*—you professor!" "What the fuck is *prevaricate?*" On the other hand, when she came out with words and phrases that I would previously have found annoying—*nucular, winduh, y'all, gimme, might could, pretty bad off*—I was reluctant to say anything because there were so many, and I didn't want to seem superior. Of course, I got used to it all, and before long, I was using some of her words myself.

"Let's try some lesbian socials," Linda suggested, and we went to Breakfast at Chaffin's. It was a monthly gathering for women forty and older. Entering the faded '50s diner serving big breakfasts, we passed a long bar to a back room where about twenty women sat around one big table. We found a space, and the women close by said hello but continued their own conversations. Even talkative Linda found it hard to engage them.

"They's all boring," she whispered.

But we met Holly, who ran a monthly lesbian potluck group, and she put us on the email list. At those gatherings, we separated and talked to different women. Linda went up to anyone and said, "Who are you?" I took my time, starting with just "Hi." We mingled with loud butch women, shy quiet ones, couples, singles looking for partners, and every age group. Linda came running over to me. "You gotta come and meet Jane and Phyllis."

Both of us liked the plump, happy pair. Stocky, blue-eyed Jane had her hair shaved up the back and sides. Phyllis was buxom and wide-hipped but with a tiny waist. They invited us to their home, where we met their birds. Linda and John had a Hahn's macaw and an African gray, so there was plenty of parrot talk. Later, they came to my place. We sat on a brick bench along the wall in a little courtyard outside the kitchen, but Linda soon got up and stood leaning against a large palm tree.

"Yeah, they's raccoons that spend nights up in this palm, and you should see the quail. They line up along the top of the wall."

Phyllis said, "Tell us about you two."

Linda laughed, spreading her brown arms wide so her nipples showed under the too-big boy's T-shirt. "We's opposites; we got nothing in common. Liz is a scientist at the university, and I dropped outta school at fourteen."

Jane put her hand on Phyllis's thigh as she said, "We are different, too, but I'm a Pisces, and Phyllis is a Taurus, so we are totally compatible."

Phyllis continued. "I am ruled by Venus and Jane by Jupiter."

Linda raised her eyebrows. "You believe that stuff?"

It turned out that Phyllis was passionate about reiki and chakra. Both talked a lot about channeling energy. I caught Linda's eye and thought, *I share more with Linda than with these two.*

After they left, Linda said, "Fuck that. All that woo-woo. I'd rather have just us."

"Me too." I put my arm around her and led her inside.

I realized that Jane and Phyllis were certainly closer to me than Linda in education and social class, yet I was much more in tune with Linda. We shared a similar sense of reality, despite all her different manners and mannerisms. We stood at the kitchen window looking out at the little palm courtyard. I laughed. "Let me put my hands on you and transfer some energy."

"Yeah, right."

For days afterward, Linda would imitate Phyllis with exaggeration, passing her hands over me as she shrieked a string of made-up words. With Linda, I was rediscovering the great value of silly. Linda's combination of inventing words and impersonating other people with much embellishment made both of us laugh out loud. And her howls of mirth at her own jokes seemed funny too. For me, a veil lifted, disclosing a past when I had always loved nonsense. How happy I was as a child in our very sober home to get Grandpa's crazy letters addressed to "Squizzley-wizzle." Later, my adored Reg and 1 chuckled at Edward Lear's poems as we read his whole book of nonsense aloud, taking turns to read "The Dong with the Luminous Nose" or "The Pobble Who Has No Toes." With Linda, though, I was living in absurdity. How it eased too tightly wound springs in my head and drove melancholy into distant corridors.

"Did your parents fuss over how you ate or anything?"

"Nah."

"We had a special way to hold teacups and saucers and use cake forks on little plates."

"Did ya put ya little pinky up when ya held a cup?" Linda laughed.

"Oh, sticking a little finger out would have been considered low class trying to be fancy. And we got lessons in elocution and deportment," but Linda was no longer listening.

She would lean back on my big leather sofa with her bare legs straight out in front, revealing the little white socks of her untanned ankles and feet. "My dad come from a poor family on a farm and drove a fire truck in Kentucky. I didn't know much about them. My mom was Cajun and spoke French when she was young. She must have been part black cos she had wiry hair and a big wide nose. She was the baby girl with twelve older brothers but the only one to graduate from high school. She met my dad when he was on leave from the war. Before the war, he had a son and then had a vasectomy. It was kind of sad. I found the photo of his little boy in his wallet, but he didn't know who the mother married. He could never find his son after the war."

She knew more about her mother's family. "I met one of Mom's brothers, who was a toothless, tobacco-chewing old fucker that asked me if I was a 'coon ass.' That means was I another ignorant Cajun. I knew other uncles, too, and one of them was great. He would talk with me all day and take me fishing."

NEIGHBORHOOD EVENTS WORKED BETTER than the lesbian ones. Linda seemed most at home with educated people, despite her own limited schooling. I was not a natural talker and always had the echo of Mother saying, "Darling, it's not nice to be too forward." But with Linda in tow, I was getting to know the neighbors better.

As we wandered around the desert, we spotted cotton-tail rabbits under bursage plants, Harris's hawks above, or distant bobcats. Gila woodpeckers screeched; cactus wrens squabbled. Purple martins nested in old woodpecker holes in saguaros. When we swam in the pool, the martins skimmed over the water, their beaks scooping sips. In the evening, lesser nighthawks did the same. The constant activity suited Linda's wandering mind.

And then Bill and Mindy arrived. They rented a large room at one end of my house. Bill was on sabbatical from a university in North Carolina, and I found them warm, friendly guests as we spent evenings watching bats in the moonlight. He worked on how they catch moths using radar and how moths make their own sound to confuse them. Linda was in her element with new people to talk to—telling old jokes, teasing serious Bill, and chatting for hours. One night, the four of us watched a lunar eclipse. It was a perfect desert night with night hawks flying, long-nosed bats taking sugar at the hummingbird feeders, and coyotes howling.

Linda wasn't impressed with the eclipse. "How long's this dang moon stuff gonna take? We gotta wait for the whole thing? Bill, you watchin' for them insect bats?"

We all had separate lives, though. Linda was more often at the home she and John had in a retirement resort across town. I was preparing to start an MFA degree at the university, and Bill and Mindy had other friends and engagements. Having times apart was the best way to keep everyone satisfied.

During one of Linda's intermittent visits, she came out with "I's adopted."

She had my attention immediately. "How did you find out?"

"I was nine and found tiny teeth in my dad's wallet, so I asked him, 'What are these?' and he said, 'Those are your baby teeth.' So I said, 'There wasn't a tooth fairy?' And he said, 'No tooth fairy.' It was amazing how everything seemed to change. I said, 'What about Santa Claus?' and he said, 'No Santa Claus.' In the end, I said, 'Next you'll tell me I was adopted.' Took a while, but he looked at me. 'As a matter of fact, you *were* adopted.'"

Later, her mother confirmed it: "But you was wanted,

Linda, and we are your mom and dad. People who can't have their own babies want them the most."

I was touched by her story and thought, *How different from the ancestry my mother was so proud of.* Mother loved to talk about our forebears' roles in the history of Australia—politicians, leaders, doctors, explorers. In our family, everyone knew who looked like whom, and I took it for granted that I was one of a clan that went back for generations. Mother knew no biology, but she read a lot and loved to talk about which genes we had inherited from which parent and how genes skip generations. She was convinced our family had a lot of "good" genes. By which she meant we had genes that made us better people. She loved to think my love of plants came from her father and my sister's beauty from her mother. I was moved that Linda felt able to tell me her story, and it made me feel closer to her.

How curious it was to have found myself with someone who really was my opposite, but I was also excited. I felt flexible and ready for novelty. In India, I had taken part in the Ganesh festival, when the elephant gods were dumped in the local tank, and lighting fireworks during Diwali. I had camped with twenty research colleagues in the Sahara Desert, where almost the only things that mattered were getting data, drinking water, and eating dried food with our fingers. My strict upbringing around manners was useful in England, but *pleases* and *thank yous* were often dropped in Eastern European countries, where people were much more abrupt. I could adapt to anything.

EVENTUALLY, I ASKED LINDA if she had followed up on her adoption and found her genetic parents. She was standing opposite me beside big bookshelves, clearly taking in the titles as she spoke. "Well, after Dad died, I took a course in investigative studies at a small college and then went to Galveston, where I was born. I met with a judge for adoption cases, and he give me all the papers he had and told me how to get state records in Austin."

"Isn't that unusual to get the papers so easily?"

We moved to the sofa. "Well, the old judge said he wanted to help because he knew that the attorney involved at the time was a crook. Anyway, it was easy. My birth mother was called Dorothy, and she had a ton a marriages and maybe twenty babies. Most were sold during childhood, but I was the lucky one—sold at birth. Never found out who she fucked."

We sat in silence for a while as I absorbed this bombshell. "When I found out, I didn't think being adopted was so bad. My parents loved me unconditionally, and life at home was good. Dad was funny and fun, and Mom would say, 'You is our gift from God, Linda.'"

"How is it that John puts up with you having lesbian affairs?"

"We been married so long and have just about everything in common. We just need each other, and John told Mom he would always be there for me."

"Well, what was so special about him back at the beginning?"

She thought for a while as she looked vacantly at the concrete floor. "I knew I was a lesbian when I was very young, but I couldn't tell anyone. I dated boys, but I was in love with an older girl called Caroline, and we had a lot of fun. She wasn't a lesbian, though, so it was pretty sad. I was fourteen when me and John became friends. I adored him."

"Adored him?"

"Yeah—we were both misfits."

John's parents were divorced, and he became almost part

of her family, spending evenings and weekends with them. The interdependence grew intense.

"After John got a job with Texas Instruments, I had time to spend with women I was attracted to, but my love for them was never returned, and John never knew I was a lesbian. When I got to twenty-one, we were just expected to marry, and I knew I wanted to stay friends with him. The night before the wedding, I was outside, and Mom found me crying. She said, 'Caroline will never be there for you.' She must have known I was gay but never said."

They went to rock concerts, smoked a lot of pot, took their boat out fishing, and worked on craft jobs at their house. "John bought me a new car every year. I was dead scared of getting pregnant and made him get a vasectomy. We shopped together at Mervyns and bought identical golf shirts and shorts. Summers we went to Colorada in an RV."

John only discovered Linda was a lesbian after she had an affair with Kim, just a year before we met at Wingspan. When Kim broke it off, Linda was so distraught that John told her he was okay with her finding another woman. I had met a lot of people with unusual life circumstances in academia, but this was new. Now I had a lover whose husband didn't seem to mind her lesbian relationships.

On top of all the differences we discovered, there was little overlap in our personal tastes. She laughed at how little I knew about rock or country music, though she knew a lot of classical music if it had been used in movies. She also loved cars. My ignorance about them amused her.

Once, we passed a gas station, where Linda pointed. "Look, a Porsche!"

"Where?" I replied, though I was not really interested.

"See that?" she said, pointing to a silver sports car.

"Oh, just a sports car," I said.

"My god, it's a Carrera!"

"You mean it's not a Porsche?" I replied, delighted.

"Oh god, babe, it's a Porsche Carrera. You don't know nothing, do ya?"

When it came to food, I knew she loved seafood and disliked anything foreign or "foo-foo." She had little concept of my predilection for all the Indian, Chinese, French, or Spanish foods. I had lived an international life and spent hundreds of evenings with Reg in cafés all over Europe. I loved spending an evening over a few glasses of wine, but I was prepared to go along with what was required for the time being: very simple food eaten quickly.

I said to Linda, "Your kind of eating is like filling up at a gas station."

"Yeah," she replied casually. She clearly didn't think that was disparaging.

Linda's past included softball, golf, fishing, and RV camping, whereas mine was hiking and wilderness camping. She liked safety, and I liked adventure. Our lack of compatibility didn't lend itself to a long-term relationship, but I was discovering her. It was an adventure unto itself.

Christmas came, and I flew off to Australia to visit relatives for three weeks. On the plane, I dreamed of the days when I first knew Reg and how his plain flat face with a mole on one cheek could make my day sparkle. How his smile with a slightly prognathous jaw was lovelier than that of any handsome man. There was that day when we sat in Bloomsbury Square in London after lunch and a beer at the Gloucester Arms. He turned to my admiring face, and our lips met. The stories of intense love had been a chimaera until then. Leaves of shrubs turned to luminous jade, and the crystal, chilly air filled with specks of diamond light. All the years that followed brought us ever closer. And I developed a warm relationship with Philip and Anne, the two children from his earlier marriage.

But I missed Linda in the hot Brisbane days, and I scribbled verses, but they never seemed quite right for her: she was more into limericks.

THE NEW YEAR'S REUNION when I returned from Australia was joyful. Waiting for my luggage at the airport, we twirled round and round together as Linda regaled me with stories of all that entertained her in my absence. Six months had passed since Linda and I had met, and distance had given us time to realize that our relationship was strange but uniquely special despite our individual needs for time apart. We had no idea what the future held.

4 Road Trip

A YEAR AFTER WE met, I was dizzy with passion for Linda. I didn't care about the future. I was ready to just try anything new. When she suggested going to Utah in her motor home, I welcomed what I would earlier have thought unappealing, never mind the strangely unplanned itinerary and unknown return time.

The first day out of Tucson, Linda decided we would camp at Dead Horse Ranch State Park near Cottonwood. Linda drove, and I was left with the maps, so arriving in the little town of Cottonwood, I said, "It looks as though you need to take the next one to the northwest, go three miles, and maybe turn on Tenth Street."

Linda looked at me as the words spurted out. "You need to circumvent the parallaxes and intercept at the peripheral."

I smiled and put down the map, but she found the way with an uncanny sense of direction. The park, with fast-flowing Verde River lined with cottonwood trees and willows, was grassy green and quiet. Linda disconnected her tow truck and perfectly backed the motor home into its numbered site under a mesquite tree as I admired the shady, spacious lot.

"Babe, come and see. Here's where you plug in the power. Now you unroll the hose and attach it to the tap. I'll do the sewer later cos the holding tank is almost empty."

As instructed, I went inside and turned the fridge from propane to electricity, switched from pump to mains water, and ran it through the pipes. I flushed the toilet and opened the roof vents.

Leaving our kitty, Yoyo, we walked with Labrador Bailey through the mesquite forest past fishing ponds with cattail reeds to the Verde River—famous for its permanent flow through arid land, with all the accompanying wildlife.

"Look, bub, zone-tailed hawk!"

Linda looked at me. "Oh, babe, I's too excited for birds. Just us for *weeks*! I got you all to myself!"

I looked at my smiling, boyish lover in knee-length cargo shorts and old golf shirt. How I loved that animation!

Suddenly, Bailey jumped into a muddy flume. "Bailey, get outta there, or y'all get karma sutra."

"Giardia?" I laughed and threw a stick over Linda's shoulder.

She ducked. "Son of a bitch, I thought it was a snake. Scared the fuck outta me."

I looked at her. Almost anything would scare the fuck outta her.

Later, she put steak on the grill, and I sat watching her, a silhouette in the setting sun.

"I'm freezin'," complained Linda. But as we began eating, she said, "I'm burnin' up."

I was used to Linda's trains of thought about tummy take, booboo, spasm, or painful finger. She even admitted, "I's a wuss."

Next morning, we had lesser goldfinches at the seed feeder we had hung in our overhanging mesquite. Linda watched them. "Hey, they's good at taking off the outside of the seeds."

I smiled to myself, remembering how I had once tried to tell her about their habits, and she had shouted, "It's just a little yella bird."

Suddenly, "Sorry for that."

I looked at her questioningly.

"Sorry about the fortuitous, but a breeze, so you couldn't smell it."

It took a minute for me to realize she referred to a fart. Earlier, she had used the word *elevator* to describe a fart because she'd once expelled one in an elevator. After a bathroom trip, she would sometimes shrug. "Just elevator."

From Cottonwood, we drove to Glen Canyon. As we slowly crossed the dam, an array of cliffs came into view, with the waters of Lake Powell extending into every nook and cranny of what was once, according to David Brower in *Let the River Run through It*, a hundred paradises. Dozens of giant steel pylons with high-tension wires stood as industrial ornaments on the red, rocky heights. I had read Edward Abbey and listened to Richard Shelton read his poems about Glen Canyon. Clearly it was one of those places that should have been preserved, though I had no concept of its glory before the dam—before the making of Lake Powell. Across from us, above the water, a 140-foot-high bathtub rim of white salty deposits marked the high-water level from years earlier, and above that, towering cliffs rose, pink and red in the late sun.

"Gorgeous," I whispered.

"Holy fuck!" shouted Linda.

We made our way down from the dam to treeless Wahweap campground with the expansive view of craggy mountains, sheer cliffs, canyons, and islands before us and settled into a site with a 180-degree panorama of the lake.

"You know they's not American if they don't reply when you say hi," Linda noted after returning from a walk around the campsite. "Let's take the kayaks out."

We drove to the water's edge. "You hold the front end there while I unhook the back." Eventually, we had both kayaks down from the truck and paddled out toward a mountain of rock rising from the lake. I raced ahead as Linda called, "You's hawlin' ass, you little circumfiction. Let's paddle round the big-ass rock then." We circled round big-ass Lone Rock and into a cove that led to a series of complicated structures: long finger inlets, the rock faces with strangely rounded humps covered in holes, caves with layers of ledges, slopes with ridges like ripples in sand. Finally, blisters developing, we paddled slowly back across the bay.

"Fuck, I'm tired."

"Me too." I put my arm around Linda. "Let's go and eat."

That evening, arm in arm, I told her about working in Nigeria on agricultural pests. "It was a lot of fun because the Nigerians were always joking, and we loved working with them. There were very few white people where we worked, though, and I found out what it's like to be a minority person."

Linda described something of her past in Dallas. "I always had cameras and got the shots, like drowned kids pulled out of a car and houses burning down with people trying to jump from windows. I was freelance. Sold photos to AP and publishers. Attorneys paid the best. You shoulda seen some a' the others. Julie, so particular her shit didn't stink; dumpster-diving Paul. Sharon, she was a blowjobby type."

Linda settled to play on her iPad, and I began reading *Travelers' Tales: Grand Canyon*, an anthology of essays by authors who loved the place. But it wasn't long before we were ready for bed. Linda held me close.

"Your eyes are like turds floating in a liquid cesspool," she crooned, and we fell over laughing on the bed, kicking off the sheets. Linda was fascinated by my eyes, which are green with brown spots. We kissed, and I ran my hand through her black crew cut and over her round, suntanned face.

"I grub you, bub."

"I grubs you too, babe."

As she slept, I marveled at the different life I was living and at Linda, who loved the weird professor. She delighted in making me laugh with crazy talk that flowed more riotously on this trip than at home in Tucson. Here, uncertainties about her husband back in Tucson and our disparate backgrounds were tempered by the simplicity of a twosome, Linda in charge.

The next day, with Bailey, jackets, fishing gear, and cooler, we raced full throttle in a rented powerboat out across the bay and toward the dam. It was Linda's birthday, and her eyes shone with the love of water and speed, the remnants of Glen Canyon towering above.

She smiled and said slowly, "Fuuck."

I thought briefly. "Why *fuck*?"

"Is good fuck," she laughed. "You's so cute."

We slowed in the narrows of Antelope Canyon. Linda had the fishing poles, hooks, plastic worms, lures, flies, plastic jerk baits, and, most importantly, frozen anchovies. Ignoring me, who knew nothing of fishing but felt real bait was needed, she left the anchovies untouched.

"This was an amazing hydroelectric project after the flooding of Glen Canyon."

"Can't be symposius when I'm trying to fish."

I was silenced, but like most of her made-up words that rolled so fast out of her mouth, *symposius* curiously fit the moment.

Then, at last, "Let's try them albatross, babe."

While she worked one fishing pole with lures, I gave her an anchovy for the other, and she left it hanging over the stern. Bailey and I lay idly on the floor of the boat.

"Shit, babe, look at that albatross pole." It was bending at the tip, and she dropped the other pole, grabbed the anchovy one, took in the slack, yanked it skyward, and reeled it in.

"Shit, I got one! Oh, babe, look! Son of a bitch, look at 'er. Get the net . . . hurry."

Two feet of fighting silver dangled above the glittering water, and I rushed for the net. "Sons of bitches, without that net, we'd a' lost 'er. See how the hook is nearly through 'er lip? Look at 'er, babe. Look at the lovely striper. It's made my day! What a birthday! Thank you, babe. Quick, take my picture with 'er. I so happy, babe. Now for another striper!"

I watched in admiration until her excitement abated and then lay down in the bottom of the boat in my long-sleeved shirt and big hat as I peeled an orange. Not wanting to interrupt Linda, I talked instead to Bailey: "How's my Bailey-boo? You my big baby, my wussy puppy."

"Bub, you want some orange?"

"No orange, babe; that's how I keep my body swelft."

Which made me think of Linda's passion for chocolate.

She cleaned the fish at a cleaning station, but I had to cook. "You gotta do southern style." I dipped the filets in cornmeal and deep fried them. We were settling into different roles.

I enjoyed Lake Powell and Linda's love of water, boats, and fishing but was ready for more of nature and canyons, less of people and dams. At our next campsite near Bryce Canyon, we sat among the ponderosa pines, watching Clark's nutcrackers forage for dog kibble we had scattered. Linda took her camera out as I sat writing on my laptop, happy with the temporary simplicity of life. Linda was happy for me to just be there, bending over to kiss me or sitting beside me at the picnic table with an arm around my waist. She chuckled that one of the stories I was writing would be about her.

"I sit with the stenographer, and she write down all my symposium."

After a short silence, "We should've went to Zion."

"Maybe I need some time alone," I snapped.

"You have no symphony for me. Usually, you so gratuitous and grateful with your time, and I always in your despair."

I looked at her tenderly. Mollified, Linda set up the tripod and sat waiting for the great bird photo. It didn't take long to see something.

"Look, babe. Quick, come 'ere."

"What?"

"Can't you see that sucker?" She had spotted a mountain chickadee I had missed.

We lazed through the morning with Bailey and Yoyo, but by midday, we were ready to leave the campsite and see the great cities of towering rocks at Bryce Canyon. I had never been there, and I walked cautiously to a canyon rim to look down at all the hoodoos. And plants.

"Come look at this tiny flower in the family Asteraceae," I beckoned from the cliff edge.

"Sons of bitches, you come over here," Linda yelled urgently.

I obeyed, and she put her arms tight around me. We walked hand in hand, sun highlighting patches with gold and shadows enhancing the complex architecture of the hoodoos. We stopped at intervals: "Gotta shoot that!"

Later, back at the campsite, Linda spotted the Texas license plate of the camp host. She couldn't pass that up. "Hi, where y'all from in Texas?" she asked a big, bearded guy. "Used to fish at Galveston. Yeah, all along the coast. Any good fishing round here?"

"Sure, there's a good lake up the road north'a here. Go over the crossroads, and you'll find Pine Lake. Rainbows and browns there, easy. Great place. Get the paste bait at Ruby's."

So we planned on Pine Lake next day as we ate grilled steak once more. Suddenly, Linda coughed violently, and I rushed to pat her on the back.

"I's okay. Got caught on my hangy-down guy. You just woofing it down, aren't cha?"

She always needed dessert to follow, but we had no sticky coffee cake or shocking-pink cupcakes. The plain chocolate we brought would have to do.

Suddenly, Yoyo began climbing on the screen door and hanging onto the wire.

"Bub, she's having trouble disengaging her claws," I called.

"*Disengaging?* Oh, babe, you want to make a grapht out of it? A spreadsheet? You always with pearls of wisdom on your oyster tongue."

We held each other laughing, a hug that quickly turned into a passionate embrace.

The next day, we explored the rocky scenery in earnest. My preference was for the sights and sounds of nature and a walk of a few miles at least. Linda, though, cared little for long walks. "Such pain in my laygs. My knees killing me."

I kept longer walks for early morning while she slept, when I could grasp the solitude and absorb the mystic whisperings of wilderness.

That evening, in bed early, Linda leaned over. "What's that book?"

"Essays—nature stuff and travel sort of thing."

"Well, read some to me. That'll put me to sleep."

I looked for a passage that could be read out of context and began in the middle of *Gone Back to Earth* by Barry Lopez: "We re-board three large rubber rafts, and enter the Colorado's quick, high flow. The river has not been this high or fast since Glen Canyon dam. Jumping out ahead of us, with its single oarsman and three passengers, is our fourth craft . . ."

Interrupted by loud laughter, I looked at Linda rolling in the bed with her legs kicking. "Craaaft, raaaft, you so fancy smancy, so Eengleeshy, so very queenie."

I am comfortable with myself and all my defects real and imagined, so Linda's teasing was just funny. "Always you tease me," I gasped as we fought with pillows.

"Yes, I a-teasa you, I teasa you, you little contigenera, you professor doctor." She grabbed me into her arms. Whether it was the reading, the exhaustion of laughter, or simple weariness, she quickly fell asleep, allowing me to finish the essay and ponder Lopez's final thoughts in relation to the splendid scenes we had witnessed in recent days.

> The living of any life, my life, involves great and private pain, much of which we share with no one. In such places as the Inner Gorge, the pain trails away from us. It is not so quiet there, or so removed, that you can hear yourself think, that you would even want to; that comes later. You can hear your heartbeat. That comes first.[*]

---

[*]   Quote from Barry Lopez book, *Crossing Open Ground*, by Barry Lopez, 1989, Vintage Books.

My private pain was never shared. But as Lopez writes, the special places ease it without thinking. As for hearing my heartbeat, having Linda with me meant the intervals were few but precious. It was in the hours of silent darkness or the birdsong early mornings that I lived the special moments alone, to hold the places of solace to me, to hear their balm.

IT ONLY TOOK AN hour at Pine Lake, surrounded by alpine meadows with high mountains beyond, to catch four rainbow trout. I had never seen Linda so relaxed and happy in Tucson and wondered about the future while she complained: "Oh, my thumb so sore where that fishhook went in. Toxins vacillated into my cubicles."

As we were leaving Bryce, Linda went into hyper mode: "Look at them Dutch! Look, midgets—look at that girl's shorts tucked into her fat butt crack! Need tweezers to pull them out! Look, bunny! There's a Texas license plate. Look, they got a Jesus thing by their motor home." I couldn't keep up with her long litany of rapid observations, but I looked at Linda's face full of fun, vision rushing ahead of her thoughts.

On so many occasions, Linda had commented about other people. Often, she could be interpreted as mean-spirited. Shocking even. But for me, the brutally honest or artless statements in the manner of a six-year-old were surprisingly refreshing. It was often done with unusual verbiage and much laughter, and I was ready for laughter, glad of Linda's ingenuous spontaneity.

The road meandered northeast along byways of red cliffs and boulders, white rock canyons dotted with the dark green pines, to Capitol Reef National Park. The motor home struggled up hills, and at the high pass over Boulder Mountain, we stopped to walk among aspens dressed in quivering new greens with the white, black-lined trunks. I examined my first green gentians, greenish white flowers on tall stalks. I felt a spontaneous passion for the perfection of each flower's symmetry: four petals dotted with purple, a bunch of stamens tipped with purple pollen lying against each petal, and four yellow-tipped stigmas, each one between two petals. Kneeling, I resisted the urge to touch something so perfect or desecrate it with talk.

"Get me some chocolate," Linda commanded when we were back on the road.

I smiled at her bossiness. "You are incorrigible."

"Yes, I always incognito. I need chocolate."

As she drove, I left the passenger seat for the kitchen cabinet and selected four Hershey's nuggets. I unwrapped them and handed each to Linda as she kept her eyes on the road. She smiled. "We will be at Capitol Reef tomorrow."

"BABE, OUR BOY IS so droopy we gotta get to a vet. And I got a huge headache. What a clusterfuck" were Linda's first words early the next day. And so followed a grim seventy-mile dash to Torrey, where there was a vet. Through a threatening storm and along narrow country roads we sped, over mountains, and through small towns as I lay holding Bailey on the bed at the back of the motor home. I don't remember the ailment, but antibiotics worked wonders for our beloved Labrador while we spent the night in grassy Sand Creek RV Park.

The following day was calm as we rested in a green valley under the great red cliffs of Capitol Reef National Park. Golden eagles glided high, and Linda, now a birder in earnest, became excited. It was to be her first day of making lists.

"Oh my god, those goldens, babe!"

We sat among the cottonwoods, leaves flashing silver

in the breeze and cotton fluff wafting through the air like summer snow. Bullock's orioles and Western tanagers flashed their yellows in the branches. Black-and-white hairy wood-peckers pecked the tree trunks, brown-headed cowbirds and bold American robins foraged in the grass, and an occasional chukka partridge marched across our sights. We idly watched summer as Linda ate apple pah. There we were, a sixty-five-year-old academic and a fifty-one-year-old Texas dropout—Australian egghead and fast-brained, street-smart photogra-pher with a short attention span. The one work-weary and disciplined, the other a free spirit. But we had love, and it was gentle that soft summer day. Linda held my hand tight and then kissed it gently.

"I'm an adult toddler."

"And I am a toddling adult," I replied. As I watched Linda wandering off with Bailey, I realized that her comment was revelatory. Some part of her had never grown up. Perhaps that was part of her appeal, the way one can be charmed by a chatty six-year-old. Part of her was also insecure, and I was happy she could be a buoyant leader on this trip.

We went northeast to the town of Green River, through red-and-white canyons, by gray mesas and treelined streams, to camp on the Colorado River in Moab. It was a shady site with wireless Internet, good for using computers outside.

"Fuck, I got a bug on my computer screen! What is it?"

"Just a chironomid fly."

"Yeah, I hate chrysanthemums on my screen."

I settled down to try to write.

"What chew got there, bucko?"

"Just adding some anecdotes. Nothing much, bub."

"Okay, you put in some antidotes? You just writing for your bemusement, eh?"

"Hmm."

"Talkative little chipmunk," she chided.

"Well, adios amoebas. See ya . . . wouldn't want ta bee ya." And she went off to shower.

Later, we lay in bed in each other's arms as a dust storm raged outside.

"Holy fuck, sons of bitches." It wasn't the time for me to respond that as dust storms went, it wasn't much. I held her as memories of camping in the Sahara Desert to work on grasshopper flight activity ran before my eyes: how we waited in Land Rovers as dust rolled past for hours and later put the tents back up. My so-different life swept back from the corners of consciousness, with all the giddy feelings of exciting field work. But I needed to take off the professor's hat, forget the bittersweet nostalgia, and savor this new life and love.

"Talk to me, babe," Linda pleaded.

How could I explain my complex emotions? My youthful past and all the work with Reg in Mali or Niger, a lifetime of research with an adored colleague and lover. I said simply, "I love you."

Arches National Park was the most photogenic place of all, and we both took hundreds of photos of distant vistas and cliff views through red-rock arches. "Fuck, babe, this is the best," Linda said, but later, she somehow lost her photos. Without them, it was as if she had never been there, and she never wanted to talk about Arches or ever again mention our great day there.

Finally, the high plateau of pristine Canyon Lands National Park offered vast vistas of etched red rock, angular cliffs, and dry waterways. We trailed quietly along a narrow path, and silently I enjoyed sego-lilies' white petals with yellow bases. We were both still recovering from the exhilarating but terrifying drive up a long one-lane back road, with cliffs dropping a thousand feet right beside us round the switchbacks. At every turn, we had feared a car coming down the one-lane road, and we had to rest at the top to recover. The great vistas are now remembered mostly by looking at the photos.

Toward home, the road south became flatter with occasional terraced statues of red, the last remnants of strata not yet weathered away. Gray sagebrush took the place of the darker greens of juniper and pinyon pine until, finally, the red earth was barren. Back in Arizona, we climbed into the White Mountains to Fool's Hollow Lake Recreation Area, full of piney smells. Above the lake, ospreys soared, and Linda got her prize photo.

In bed, Linda had her iPad for a game of poker, and I opened a new book, Aldo Leopold's *A Sand County Almanac*. Then lights out and the comfort of skin on skin before sleep.

I got up early. From the picnic table, long early-morning shadows of pines pointed toward the blue lake and rocky bank beyond. Doing nothing, I was learning to give up my ties to the academic life and write my story. Most of it would be done when I was alone.

Linda appeared as a black-headed grosbeak landed nearby, and her newfound birding spirit soared. "Is that cool or what?" I felt a strange melting whenever her bird-delight took wing.

"Bublet, I love you."

"I love you too, babe."

We lazed through the morning. Linda—tanned, young-looking in her boy's shorts—waited for birds to photograph. She moved my chair into the shade at intervals. She tried not to talk as I wrote.

The next day when we set off for home, Linda said, "Sad."

"Why sad?"

"Because coming to an end."

The trip had been a complete break for her from the complication of a life shared with two people—John, her husband of over thirty years; and me, a woman lover she had pined for all her life.

But I was not sad—the trip would become another collection of tender memories when each of us had been on a remarkable high, thinking only of the uncomplicated present and our affection for each other as we explored Utah. And of all the close partnerships I had observed through my life, one factor stood out in the best ones: an ability to laugh at everything and everybody but especially at and with each other. We had plenty of that.

5 Reflections

SHADOWS OF FEATHERY LEAVES quivered on the concrete as I sat under the Chilean mesquite tree on my patio in Tucson. A Gila woodpecker squawked in one of the high branches. Looking beyond the low stone patio walls to the south, two tall saguaros rose above the prickly pear, cholla and bursage. I was lucky to have had sixteen years surrounded by this rich ecosystem, little changed for thousands of years. I rested there after three weeks' travel with Linda, thinking of how extraordinary it had been.

We laughed so often in Utah that the burden of loss I carried since Reg died had subsided. Much of the comedy depended on Linda's tone of voice, a gift for mimicry and wry facial expressions. Trying to copy her would be an embarrassing failure. But I had written Linda's crazy words and phrases in a notebook, and often they inscrutably communicated meaning the way a kaleidoscope's multitude of glass pieces made unexpected patterns. How did she select from what seemed to be a vast reservoir of miscellaneous items in her brain? And how did riotous meaning come out of her mouth with such lightning speed?

I WANTED ANSWERS, BUT all I could be sure of was our differences. In school, I was slow to learn and was still interpreting what I heard from teachers long after others came up with answers to their questions. Playing tennis, I could hit the balls that bounced but was too slow to succeed at the net. My worried mother took me to the new vocational guidance office in Brisbane when I was thirteen. After an IQ test, I sat waiting with her in a small, hot room. Mother's trifocals steamed up and sweat gathered behind my knees. A thin, bespectacled psychologist walked in looking serious. He sat opposite us and leaned forward for his long speech. I recall little. But there was one sentence that confirmed my worst fears, and I can still remember it: "There are anomalies, but Elizabeth's score overall is subnormal, and she should consider shorthand and typing for a career."

I had been paralyzed by the pressure for a quick answer at each test, my young bare legs sticking to the metal chair and my mind going blank as the tester sat impassively at a window opposite me, staring at my every move. The year ahead was one of misery and self-doubt. But then I fell in love with the math teacher, who wouldn't tolerate failure and inspired me to succeed. How lucky I was then to have other teachers who believed in me and told me I could do anything. They changed my life. The slow brainchild eventually won a scholarship to the University of Queensland.

By contrast, Linda was aware of being very smart from an early age.

"Yeah, I rushed through all the IQ tests and always got a high value, like a hundred and sixty. In class, I finished stuff quickly and could sit at the back of the class and play."

Her boredom with classes added to her dislike of school, where she was seriously bullied. She told me she was happy to leave in eighth grade because she never seemed to fit in. Yet she had the fastest brain I had ever come across and loved to amuse me with wild wordplay and off-the-wall phrases.

Once when my friend Nancy was visiting, Linda wickedly imitated people she had known, with imagination enhancing reality to great effect.

Nancy chuckled quietly. "You should do standup."

"Oh no, I ain't doing stuff in fronta people."

Linda could also cut anyone down to size in an instant, and she made fun of me for being slow. My life has been so good and my career successful, so her comments were nothing but fun for me. That she teased me meant she was focused on me. I felt it was a sign of affection. But it was speed that astonished most. Timing and especially speed make the funniest standup comedy performances, as San Francisco writer Tony Hicks noted when describing comedian Robin Williams as having the "fastest brain on the planet." But there are advantages to being slow. Linda's wordplay could be too fast for self-editing, too fast to avoid faux pas.

As I grew older, I became increasingly convinced that slow was fine, so reading Tara Kadioglu was gratifying. In the *Boston Globe*, she wrote about how we remember the story of the tortoise and the hare, but few of us have learned the lesson it teaches—slowness wins: "So-called slow thinking requires more disciplined thought and yields more productive decision-making than quick reactions and is inching its way into interventions in fields as disparate as criminal justice, sports, education, investing, and military studies."*

I think of the best responses to arguments afterward, and I learned early to reflect a little before speaking. Perhaps thinking unhurriedly about my research was part of my academic

---

* Tara Kadioglu, *The Boston Globe* July 15, 2015.

success. In my life's work as an entomologist, I learned the extraordinary value of being observant, of patiently watching animals, and even imagining myself as the creature of interest. I loved watching plague locusts and recording behaviors to answer questions about food preferences, attentiveness, and avoidance of risk. When there was a gap in their activities, I developed ideas and hypotheses about what the behaviors meant in an ecological or evolutionary context. Most of my original and creative ideas in research came to me at such times.

With all that I have learned taking an introspective approach to animal behavior, I know the work is best suited to slower thinkers who mull over and reflect on what they see, and the same is true in many disciplines. Darwin and Einstein both described themselves as slow thinkers. And it is well documented that high IQ or fast brain processing are not predictors of creativity or insight. As a professor, I had great students who were slow but thoughtful and innovative. I also had fast-brained students whose talents lay elsewhere. Linda would have been one of them, though she would not have had the patience for behavioral studies.

Linda had a career that was successful because of her incomparable speed at seeing, predicting, and acting. It had nothing to do with patience, contemplation, or thoughtfulness. She missed out on formal education, but she found a niche that suited her distinctive abilities. Being a freelance photojournalist with the fire departments in Dallas, Linda benefited from speed. She could take in the scene, quickly anticipate the next critical events, and get the winning picture. Somehow, she would be there at the dramatic or poignant moment at a fire or an accident and knew instinctively when she had the shot. She showed me a few of her favorites, like a screaming child covered in blood being cut out from a crushed Ford and the firefighter shouldering a limp woman as he backed down a ladder engulfed in flames.

Linda became part of first-responder groups where she lived in Dallas. They respected her ability to rush in, catch the action, and get a newsworthy picture. The firefighters gave her a set of firefighting bunker gear and a first responder ID card, which meant that law enforcement never interfered with any action she took to get a photo. Who knows where her abilities would have taken her if she had gone to college? Her brain speed and vast compendium of information acquired through books and TV would at any rate make her a winner on shows like *Jeopardy!*

Linda and I also differed in what we saw as funny and in the kind of jokes we each made. Much of the difference was about speed. My jokes were dry and infrequent, but Linda tested me with her jokes to see if I laughed, and she found it amusing if I didn't get them quickly.

"I'm the funny one," she'd say.

Linda grabbed the *New Yorker* when it came. "Gotta see the cartoons."

She turned the pages quickly, laughing at intervals: "Look at this—hilarious. Do you get that?"

I read the articles that were too long to hold her attention.

Sometimes she tested me when we were watching TV. Once there was a weaselly-looking woman being interviewed in her home. Linda said, "What sort of dog do you think she has?"

I looked at the woman's face and thought how people sometimes look like their dogs. "Dachshund?"

"Try again."

"Dunno."

"Look at her bookshelf."

Behind her was a lineup of books about pugs. I hadn't noticed.

We sat in a café in Santa Fe, New Mexico, eating fajitas, and I was absorbed by my hot cast-iron dish, its flavors of chicken, onion, and pepper, oblivious to our surroundings. Linda liked the food, too, but she was eavesdropping.

"Did you hear that woman right over there in the yella dress? They called her Judy. She's in the music department at the University of Arizona. She's an asshole."

She had quickly googled the woman's college and department on her phone. "She teaches theory, whatever that means. And she got terrible student evaluations. Yeah, and she likes organ music. Plays the piana."

I looked over at the yellow dress. The woman wearing it was with three men and seemed to be doing all the talking, but I wasn't particularly interested in people I was unlikely ever to meet. I had noticed the young couple at the table next to us leaning into one another with serious expressions and felt mildly curious. "What do you think about them?"

"They's arguing about her mom, who's a Mormon that doesn't like how their kids are too independent."

"And the older waiter with a mustache over by the bar?"

"He was telling that old man by hisself what posole is."

Linda could detect and decipher multiple conversations simultaneously, and I realized that she absorbed multiple inputs most of the time.

When Linda drove, she saw beyond the cars and lights: "Look, someone bought that building; there's a crazy guy with a Portuguese Water Dog—yeah, an Obama dog; oh, a Porsche; look up there—that's a seven-three-seven . . . gotta be Southwest Airlines; hey, see the Cooper's hawk on the pole?"

On the way home from our Utah trip: "See the jackrabbit

way over there? I think they's six ravens up ahead, and guess what? One-a them's flying upside down. Look, a dead coyote. Skunk roadkill."

Meanwhile, I had seen a lone Gambel oak and was absorbed with why there was only one and whether it may be a genotype with needs suited only to this area. My thoughts were not on the broad visual input. They went to curiosity about meanings.

In *Thinking Fast and Slow*, psychologist Daniel Kahneman talks of "System 1" processes, which are quick and more or less intuitive, like driving a car on an empty road; and "System 2" processes, like parking in tight spaces, which take more time and are more reasoned or logical. Everyone, including Linda and me, uses both systems but at different times.

I tended to be more accurate than Linda. And there was also the question of focus. Linda had attention deficit disorder. There was so much activity in her brain that she didn't pay attention to anything for very long. She switched from topic to topic, so I was often confused. The slower and fewer processes in my brain at any one time allowed me to focus on the scales of a butterfly wing, the genetic control of all those colors, the great mimicry of a tasty butterfly looking exactly like a bitter or toxic one.

Exactly how quickly visual and auditory information is perceived and relayed to the brain ranges from unusually fast to so slow that it is considered a disability. Linda and I were at different points along this continuum. There is clearly a tradeoff between speed of processing and in-depth thinking, between constant acute awareness and contemplation. Sensory/neural hyperactivity can lead to fast decisions, while contemplative reflection or even unconscious thinking can result in eureka insights. Leaders of many companies that depend on staff to think creatively know this. Apple and Google workers, for example, are offered meditation rooms and yoga classes; others provide opportunities for physical activity like table tennis, recharge rooms, and even nap rooms. For me, those hours of watching animals doing not much or my solitary walks allowed my brain to drift and hit upon ideas. Even mopping the floor and cleaning the kitchen gave me the mental freedom to go somewhere imaginatively.

I came across a blog by the psychiatrist Ellen Braaten, who wrote in 2017 about her fast-paced world compared with that of her slower twenty-one-year-old son. Beyond how similar they were as mother and son, she noted how very different they were in how quickly they take in and handle information. She writes:

> I speak fast and always have too much to say and love having a lot going at one time. He likes to do one thing at a time and do it well. I apologized to my son for not planning a lot of stuff besides making dinner when he visited, and he said, "Mom, making dinner *is* doing stuff." Those with a slower speed of processing have their own skills, have a more thoughtful approach to life. They know how to slow down and be intentional. They can show us how to savor something as simple as preparing a family meal together.

Such affirmations of slowness were satisfying. They also made me more conscious of how different Linda and I really were. Perhaps there would never be more substantial elements in our relationship than the contrasts in brain speed and all the fun that it entailed. Maybe we would never cement a togetherness beyond jokes and laughter and passion. The all-consuming humor did fill our time together, but perhaps that was because we spent half of our time apart.

6 Disparity

"I ALWAYS WANTED TO be with a woman, but I can't leave John. He's my only family." She had said it several times in that first year, and I accepted that Linda would be a part-time lover. With the death of Reg still on my mind, it was hard to imagine being full-time with someone so different anyway. A half-time liaison seemed to meet the moment—Linda times for engagement in the exciting and curious present.

I needed time alone for my memories, and I needed long, solitary walks in my beloved desert to provide peace and inspiration for each day. In 1788, Jean-Jacques Rousseau wrote about walks and was one of the first writers to rhapsodize on their soothing value and the way they help our thinking and calm our spirits.

> Never did I think so much, exist so vividly, experience so much, never have I been so much myself as in the journeys I have taken alone and on foot. There is something about walking that stimulates and enlivens my thoughts. The sight of the countryside, the pleasant succession of views, the open air . . . all serve to free my spirit, to lend a greater boldness to my thinking, so that I can combine them, select

them and make them mine as I will, without fear or restraint.[*]

In the rich Sonoran Desert, my walking helped lift me from melancholy. Each day, I recorded my findings and thoughts after early-morning outings: a hot, dry presummer and then the first monsoon rain that caused swarms of leaf-cutter ants to rise in columns like smoke rose above the creosote bushes, migrating birds like the brown-and-red rufous hummingbirds on their way back from Alaska to Mexico in late summer, winter ice diamonds dripping from cactus spines early in the morning, chocolate-winged Harris's hawks calling across the tall saguaros. And often, somewhere else in my head, was Linda. How strange it was to have fallen for someone who spoke a different language, whose disparate life and interests bore no resemblance to mine. The freshness was intriguing, the novelty alluring. Yet the peculiarity of our relationship made me wary of wanting anything permanent or long-term. I didn't imagine Linda would ever enter the inner reaches of who I was, the person who valued solitude, a secret life of nostalgia, an obsession with nature.

I had no idea about Linda's life with John at the resort where they lived. She stayed with me for a couple of days most weeks, longer in summer when her resort friend Bobbi was back home in Michigan. In my desert paradise, we gradually became more used to each other. We watched javelinas trotting in high heels and cottontail rabbits lounging in the shade of a mesquite tree, always on the lookout for coy-

---

[*]   This quote is from an unfinished book by Jean-Jacques Rousseau called *Reveries of a Solitary Walker*. It was translated into English by Peter France (1980), printed by Penguin Books, quoted from the 1980 English edition.

otes loping by. We walked my backstreet circuit and laughed at neighbor Larry McMurtry's need to carry a stick against mountain lions. Would he talk about that in his revised *Lonesome Dove*? We swam in the pool as purple martins swooped for a sip. We lay on the flat roof after dark, looking at the stars.

"You the professor, eh, with all them books? Can't believe you have so much work crap at home."

"It was my life."

"Why didn't you do something interesting instead of stupid bugs?"

She had said it before, but it came out of her sparkling face with a grin, and I smiled. She loved to try to shock to see if I laughed. She looked all over my house and into all my cupboards and found my collection of tapes and DVDs. "Fuck, you got a ton a' symphony crap. I like that Ninth Symphony a' Beethoven though. Look, Itzhak Perlman, the one with the legs."

I rarely expressed the astonishment I felt. How was it that she possessed so much general knowledge when she left school in eighth grade? How did she know Itzhak Perlman with his leg braces and crutches? Why did she and John really stay together? What was she passionate about?

She brought a jigsaw puzzle and upended it on the dining table. We poked through the pieces. I found the red chimney. Can you see yellow flower pieces? But putting it together was intermittent as we stood on either side of the table by the windows looking out on the desert and Santa Catalina Mountains. "Look at them javelina; they's got a baby. Hey, a boy quail flew up into that tree."

When a Harris's hawk landed on a nearby pole, I said, "Look at him; there are five of them around here, and they hunt cooperatively."

"Cool."

I always felt an underlying suspense about what her plans might be when she came to my place. Did she even have plans? Would she be staying? Or what about the evening ahead—laughter, snuggles, and making love? She often left for the resort quite suddenly. I never knew why, but I never queried her decisions about when to come or go. I didn't want my questions to make her run away. She was still a mystery.

LINDA LOVED TO PULL my leg and laugh at habits that were different from her own.

"You's wearing granny pannies!" she shouted and screamed with laughter when she saw that I wore high briefs and not the bikini underwear she wore.

"Here," she would say, drawing her forefinger up from my chin to my lip as if collecting the dribbles of age as she laughed then kissed me. But I needed the simple nonsense.

I looked in the mirror. Usually, I don't look to see myself but rather to brush my teeth or comb my hair. One day, I looked properly. *How can she be attracted to me?* I felt a surge of love for her. She brought out a little blue notebook, and I watched as she wrote "I love you" and then passed it to me and stood back to watch my response. I rushed to embrace her and, with my arms round her neck, whispered, "I love you too, bublet." In bed, she held me tight until, of course, she couldn't resist some tickling and some teasing nonsense—anything to make me laugh.

"You procolating in my head," she announced before we went to sleep.

ONE DAY WHEN LINDA was at the resort, I looked into an

old wood chest and found bundles of ragged envelopes. I had written the letters to my mother from the time I left Australia in 1963 to her death seven years later, and my sister mailed me the whole bundle. My Waterman's fountain pen had scrawled what I thought would keep her happy and unworried twelve thousand miles away. I couldn't bring myself to open one, yet I liked having them there. We had been so close—our bond was as strong as the glue that had once closed those envelopes.

I had seen what happened when my sister left home; it would have been the same when I was gone. She listened in the mornings, waiting as she swept the floor, starched Papa's shirt collars, mended stockings, dusted the wireless, and sat at the kitchen table with the Courier Mail, drinking cups of Lipton's tea with milk. Currawongs singing in the Eucalyptus tree outside.

She would hear the postman coming up the street, his short, sharp whistles getting closer. At certain houses, he rested his bike against the fence and took a letter from a leather bag. He dropped it in a red box by a gateway and then raised the magic silver thing that hung about his neck on a thin cord. He blew his postman's whistle. Each week, her work hands unfolded a bundle of thin blue airmail sheets—but not until she had settled in that old armchair. Now these thin pages want to stay unopened in my drawer, left alone with the years. They know the eyes that read them once, twice, three times and returned to them on days without a whistle. We had shared such powerful devotion, yet I had sailed so far away. She would write back feverishly in the evenings while Papa slept his deep, unknowing sleep.

I closed the chest and walked out into the desert to see if the phainopeplas were still at the mistletoe. A group of them had set up shop in a nearby palo verde tree, and they were still there, six of them eating mistletoe berries, their quiet tweets contrasting with the squabbling cactus wrens. There was more mistletoe than the year before, and I calculated it would take just a few more years before the parasite killed the tree.

Not knowing precisely when Linda might come enhanced the excitement of her arrivals. After she had been at the resort for a few days, I was ready for the sound of her truck in the driveway—and the call, "Hey, babe," jumping down and me rushing out with, "Hello, bub" before we embraced. Then I'd glance in the window of the truck to see if she had brought an overnight bag.

I watched Linda with the tongs at the grill on my patio, tickled that I had an unconventional, amusing lover. I had the back view of her boyish figure, always in those baggy shorts, oversized T-shirt, sneakers, and little ankle socks. I contemplated her restless brown legs as she waited to turn the meat. But I was the organizer, making sure the table was arranged with knives and forks, napkins, and mats. She came in, looked at the table, and laughed—"You so formal." But she was flattered and excited by a professor's unlikely affection. She had someone who enjoyed a life of comedy and could take her teasing.

"I loves you, babe, the professor."

We visited nearby Tohono Chul Park and wandered around watching Anna's hummingbirds competing for places at the feeder or hovering as they found nectar in the red flowers of desert honeysuckle. We lingered in the palm oasis with its tiny stream and in the children's garden with a narrow waterway for toy boats. In the Sin Agua Garden, with its native plantings of corn and beans, and landscapes designed to harvest rainwater, I thought, *Must try to be less wasteful.* Linda was quick to spot an unusual torch cactus or bossy curve-billed thrasher, a hidden courtyard, a sculpture of a saguaro cactus in flower. She got restless waiting for me to read the signs on the geology wall, but she was ever aware of other people and drew attention to their peculiarities.

"Look how that old fucker's shuffling along with one foot always in front. Look at her—must be three hundred pounds—hold me back. Did you see that girl's boobs? Nipplies on high beam." The observations rolled off her tongue like a verbal explosion. That she was outrageous ignited a joyful rebelliousness I had fostered in my youth. Was it rebellion that made me leave my country and the mother who meant so much?

I realized then how much of my life had been about rebellion or at least challenging convention. Even my research career had thrived on ideas that were new and different from anything current, and what fun it had been to defy fashionable theory and follow data that was excitingly unexpected. What fun to upend hypotheses! With the joy of observation, I designed experiments in the study of why plant-feeding insects needed to specialize, as most of them do. I found that it was not about diversity of plant toxins requiring them to specialize on a few, as theory would have it—the caterpillars and grasshoppers needed to be vigilant for predators, and that was easier when attending to the few cues from one plant type rather than choosing among a myriad of plant species. Data that was new could lead to disparagement from old hands, but even that had its appeal. If my concepts eventually won the day, as they often did, my satisfaction was complete. And how grateful I had always been for Reg's love and admiration, and how we fed on each other's research ideas. I was the provocateur with the wild ideas, and he had the more careful logic.

Linda was different. I loved her and was refreshed and entertained by her. I relished the novelties she brought into my life. But Linda didn't do soulmate. There had been only one, and he remained the only one, even in death. I was molting to a new and different existence, exciting and novel, but I deeply prized the past. Meanwhile, the exhilaration of my new existence with Linda eclipsed questions about the future. I was swept along despite feeling, *This can't be real.* Linda was clearly fascinated with how different my life had been, but it was only later that I discovered she was always wondering, *How the fuck could someone like her actually care about me?*

My cat, Tigger, was clearly not fond of Linda, though. He sat in a corner for hours facing the wall whenever she showed up, and if anyone we met seemed grouchy, Linda would comment, "They's tiggering."

WHEN TROOPER, LINDA AND John's old yellow Lab died, Linda was miserable, and she said John was too; the much-loved dog had been an important part of their bond.

"You need a new puppy," I declared. I wanted their bond to remain. So John went to Colorado to pick up a two-month-old puppy, Bailey. Linda always brought her to my place. We took her for walks and swam in the pool with her, lying on float beds as she paddled around us. All three of us were happy to have Bailey: who can't enjoy a Labrador puppy?

I took Linda to a piano recital by the dramatic Chinese concert pianist Lang Lang. I had to get aisle seats—"I's claustrophobic"—but was surprised at how much she enjoyed the music.

"He's great, eh, babe. So upandown."

Brian, one of my university colleagues, was at the concert with his wife, June, and I introduced Linda to the couple. June was in the process of shaking hands with her when Linda announced in her loud Texas voice, "Well, I's disappointed cos I thought we was coming to see a panda play the piana."

June withdrew her hand as if Linda were infectious. The moment passed quickly as the lights flashed for the end of intermission, and we returned to our seats smiling. It was a story she told for years. At the next concert, we saw Brian and June in the distance.

Linda said, "We oughta stand up and wave and call out, 'Hi, June.'"

She didn't do that, but as she told the story later, she invariably added the imagined scene to the anecdote and gave every indication that it was factual. I never contradicted.

Apart from Brian and June, I had other friends who were at a loss to understand my relationship with Linda. One said to me, "But she is not an intellectual." There are many professors who have never been out of their narrow paths, never known the world beyond a university campus, only known sophisticated environments. Some of them undervalue people like Linda, and I wondered what they would have been like if they had experienced her background. Although I had a privileged beginning, I had worked in factories and on farms, studied insects with help from people at all educational levels in India and Africa, taught for years in a rough high school in England that most kids left as soon as they could. I knew that education didn't define the value of a person. Further, Linda was smarter in many ways than the average university professor.

For her turn, Linda suggested a Lindsey Buckingham concert.

"Okay, who is he, then?"

"The lead guitarist for Fleetwood Mac. Me and John saw them ages ago."

"I know about them," I said.

"How the fuck do you know them? You don't know nothing about rock."

"One of the girls in the group is the sister of a colleague I had in my London lab."

"Must be Christie. What a co-inkidink!"

She talked to everyone she encountered and always came up with something funny or silly or curious. For months after the Lindsay Buckingham concert, she told people, "You wouldn't believe that Liz had a student in England who was the brother of Christie McVie, and she doesn't even know anything about rock."

The rock concert, with its flashing lights and deafening sound, made me close my eyes for minutes at a time. Beyond the bobbing heads of the audience, I took in the decorations of the restored art deco Fox Tucson Theater—the painted columns on the walls, the red and orange painted star on the ceiling. I looked around at all the enthusiastic fans jumping up and down. Most were probably in their sixties, all of them with their phones raised.

"Look at them all taking pictures!"

"No," explained Linda, "they ain't shooting; they used to hold up their flaming lighters in the old days, and now they's holding up their phones with the flashlight instead."

Next, Linda took me to hear acoustic guitarist Leo Kottke. He played at the Temple of Music and Art, a 1927 Spanish colonial building, where the acoustics were especially good. She bought seats at the front, and he played alone.

"Just look at his fingerpicking, babe. He got Grammys for that."

I couldn't take my eyes off his racing hands on the twelve-string guitar and the sound that seemed like two or three people playing.

Like Lindsey Buckingham, Leo Kottke was in his sixties, and I realized Linda's choices reflected what she had enjoyed in her youth.

In my turn, I took her to *The Threepenny Opera*. We had good seats in the front row of the balcony at Tucson Music Hall. I was excited as I felt it was the best first opera for Linda, with a touch of jazz and German dance music. But as soon as it started and "Mack the Knife" began, I knew it would be a flop. The singing and staging were both terrible and the performance tedious. Linda was restless and looked over the railing to the stalls below.

"Lots of bald heads," she whispered. "You could spit on them."

I whispered back, "Okay, spit on the people below." Of course, we did no such thing, but she loved the idea of it. We stayed the course, by which time Linda couldn't get outside fast enough. There, a group of boys drummed on paint buckets with sticks. "Best part of the evening," she declared. As time went on, the story included, "You shoulda seen Liz spitting on the people below!"

Linda took me to my first women's basketball game, and when the home team, the Arizona Wildcats, scored a point, we made the appropriate bobcat growl and held our hands up as claws. Then I unwittingly cheered for a point made by the visiting team—a faux pas Linda never let me forget.

"Shoulda seen Liz. You wouldn't believe it, but she cheered both teams."

I laughed. I remembered how in Berkeley, when my students took me to a football game of UC Berkeley against

Stanford, a section of the crowd seemed proud that their home team was losing. Intellectual pursuits trump ball games seemed to be the idea.

The day before Linda turned fifty, she disappeared. A few days away was normal, but I wondered why she hadn't called. I waited a week. *Has she finally given up on me?* I had always braced myself for Linda's eventual departure, but I didn't expect this silent and sudden disappearance so soon. Eventually, I got anxious. *Maybe something is seriously wrong.* I called John, even though I didn't really know him.

"Lin went off in our motor home to Texas. She took Bailey."

"Well, she said nothing to me, so I got worried."

"She felt bad that she would reach the awful fifty with no one caring and no celebration, so she figured she'd go where there would be no one who could disappoint her."

She was fishing on the Gulf Coast—something she loved.

Our next meeting was awkward. "Why did you go away?"

"When John got to fifty, the resort put on a party for him. They wouldn't do it for me."

I understood her feelings and hugged her. I had been a successful scientist and ended up as a Regents Professor but only really escaped the feeling of being a fraud late in my career.

Linda loved to watch TV programs about different countries, though she wouldn't have dreamed of travel herself. She talked a lot about the countries she had seen on travel programs and movies set in different exotic places.

I said, "Let's have a trip to Hawaii."

She blinked, stared at me for a while, and then said, "I gotta go now."

She was gone for a week with no word to me. Once more, I called John.

He said with a laugh, "You'll never get her on a plane," and I was left to wonder about Linda's earlier life.

I was keen to spend some time in Australia, the land of my youth. Clearly, Linda was unlikely to join me, but she loved internet exploration, so when she did visit again, we started looking on the web at tourist attractions in Australia. "That's your home place, eh?"

"You know, I could take you there."

She laughed. After the Hawaii fiasco, she couldn't imagine I would try something even wilder. We continued looking at Australian tourist destinations on the internet, and I showed her my favorite places. Eventually, she said doubtfully, "It would be good, eh?" She was happy to continue looking at Sydney Harbour, the Great Barrier Reef, and the beaches near my hometown of Brisbane. We went to airline websites. I watched her—transfixed by the planes, their routes, and their sizes and models. She would remember all that just as she remembered all the makes of cars and motorbikes. I took the plunge: "How about going for a trip there?"

"Yeah, right," she replied caustically, knowing I couldn't be serious.

"Let's get the tickets! Really," I pressed.

She fell to her knees. I grabbed her hot, sticky hands, and she sobbed, "Nooooo."

She wanted to travel but was too nervous. I discovered she had never been on a bus or a train, let alone a plane, and realized how totally circumscribed her life had been regarding travel—cars and motor homes in a few states.

I held her. "You can do it. We will have a practice run to San Diego."

"I love you, babe, but I don't know if I can. I seen so much bad. I was at the 1985 Delta crash when a hundred and thirty-six people were killed. I's claustrophobic. I need to be in control. I's afraid of a panic attack."

She went back to the resort and, a few days later, surprised me with a phone call.

"Babe, I got two round-trip tickets to San Diego!"

I was thrilled at the excitement in her voice. Her desire to see new places had won. She continued, "I had to be the one to buy them so if I chicken out, it's my money down the drain." She hugged me and said, "I will try to get ready. I's going to a psychologist."

That didn't last more than two visits. "He just talks about hisself all the time." She settled for lorazepam.

When we got to Tucson airport, I requested preboarding passes to get seats at the front, saying that my "ward" was extremely claustrophobic. At last on the plane, she frantically looked around and then took a photo of us together in the front seats. She gazed out the window as we moved away from the terminal, and with the acceleration on the runway, she half stood. "Look! We's going up!"

"This is my first flight ever," she told each flight attendant.

Soon, she had an audience of them, and one gave her little wings to pin on her jacket. She grinned with pleasure as she attached the pin. A flight attendant came by to ask for orders.

"How's it going?" But she declined any drink, having deemed it safer to bring her own.

She was glued to the window with her camera. "Look, great photos of the mountains! There's the Pacific!" She knew the sprawling city of San Diego, where she had been with John, its wide bay enclosed by Coronado Island. Her aerial photo of the blue expanse of Mission Bay became one of the few pictures on the wall of their house.

After getting our bags, Linda marched out and got us a taxi. She seemed totally in control, yet she had never even been in a taxi before. At El Cordova, our modest hotel on Coronado Island, we were unexpectedly given an upgrade to a suite.

"Babe, an upgrade! We's getting two rooms and a kitchen." I found out then that hotels didn't figure in her life experience either. The time went quickly. The thing we both liked best was the zoo. First, the pandas: "Babe, just look at the adorable mama and baby." We walked through the jungly hillside to see the apes, where we spent the rest of the day. For hours, we watched a youthful bonobo lying on its back, holding a piece of grass above his face. He twiddled it around, apparently daydreaming. We both felt the rush of wanting to hold this engaging genetic relative.

Back on Coronado, we looked at restaurants. Most of them were unacceptable to Linda—too fancy, foo-foo, foreign. But at a simple café, she saw coconut shrimp on the menu outside.

"This the place."

"Okay."

The fish tacos I chose were bland and soggy, and we ate in silence. I thought of the gourmet meals I would not be having with Linda as images rose in my mind of chicken korma at the Emerald restaurant in Hyderabad and Spanish lamb at the Alberonia in Jerez.

"We gotta take a look at the Del," she said suddenly.

"I don't know the Del."

"Oh, babe, it's a gorgeous, big hotel here, and it's in Marilyn Monroe movies."

And so we visited the nearby lavish, wood-built Hotel

del Coronado that opened in 1888 as the largest resort hotel in the world. We sauntered around the upscale stores and along verandas with views of the bay. There were mementos of many movie stars, and I recognized the entrance with the steps down to the beach in *Some Like It Hot*.

"See, babe? Marilyn!"

We took off our shoes and walked along the beach holding hands. We took photos of our shadows and footprints and Linda's writing in the damp sand before the waves washed it away: "12-03-2005—I love you."

7   The Resort

IT WAS A WINDY day with the air full of dust as I drove to a vast, walled community of small stucco houses with an RV park for thousands. In the west, gray towers of a federal prison rose out of the desert that stretched for miles. A small gate opened out to a deserted trail through the prickly pear and creosote.

The beige house with attached garage sat close to the street, behind a few pink flowering Hesperaloe plants. Linda greeted me with a hug as I entered the living room. Windows to the street and a glass door to a tiny undeveloped courtyard provided light. A big-screen TV, bulky sofa, and massage chair dominated the central space, along with a wooden coffee table and cabinets Linda and John had built. I saw little decoration but noticed that beside the front door was a stained-glass panel displaying a coyote. A round wooden table with an unfinished stained-glass top stood at the center of the small dining space.

"Been doing that one for years but probably won't finish it," Linda declared as she wiped off some of the dust from a splendid owl with wings outstretched. Four small Mexican chairs painted with flowers surrounded the table, but it was obvious with all the clutter that they didn't use the table or the chairs. I peeped into John's little bedroom, which was also his office—a guy's messy space with clothes and magazines scattered across the floor.

In the garage, she showed me metal cabinets housing a collection of well-kept tools. One wall held her photography awards. She pulled down boxes and showed me textbooks on accidents and safety procedures that featured her photos, and from one tattered old box of papers she brought out the nomination documents for a Pulitzer Prize.

"I had the shot. It was at the big Delta airlines crash in Dallas that killed dozens. I was beaten by someone who had one of the busted Bay Bridge after the big earthquake in San Francisco. It happened the same year."

We walked the dogs along endless streets of similar houses and scattered facilities. "When we first come here, I used to get in that spa there with the old women. I was so bored I just wanted to shock them—'If you pee in here, it keeps the water temperature up'—but there was this Greek lady who knew I was always joking. She said, 'I lika you, Linda; you so funny.'"

She showed me the pools and golf course. I was more interested in the community workshops, especially the one for stained glass. A central table surrounded by benches was covered with pieces of colored glass and tools. Metal cabinets held small tools, flux, solder, and copper foil. It was there that Linda and her friend Bobbi spent a lot of time together, and I could imagine Linda chattering loudly, the center of attention.

Back at the house, Linda took me into her purple-painted bedroom. A permanently drawn blind covered the window, so it was rather dark. We lay down on a dog-eared rug on the unmade bed facing a large TV screen, and she told me more about Bobbi and her husband, Glen. They were among the many "snowbirds" who came to Tucson for the winter and always stayed in a reserved RV spot.

"Glen is great and reminds me so much of my dad. Bobbi's a devout Catholic, the mass-every-morning kind, and don't agree with people having gay relationships. Funny thing is she's got two gay sons. I knew as soon as I met them; one a' them's flaming. Bobbi doesn't know or pretends not to. We just hit it off somehow. Once she said, 'You remind me of a cross between someone with Down's syndrome and a nun I knew.'"

I squinted up at the one decoration on the wall above the TV—a long, faded photo of Galveston, where she was born. "We was all at a party here at the resort with a Mexican band, and Bobbi asked them to play 'One-Ton Tomato' [the Cuban song "Guantanamera"]. Well, me and Bobbi got up there with them and danced like crazy. John was embarrassed, and the people at the tables were kinda shocked, but they all died laughing.

"There was about twenty of us having lunch at the casino, and I says to Bobbi, 'Cut up my food,' and she leaned over and cut everything into tiny bits. You shoulda seen how all the others started looking over and nudging each other. When the dessert came, there was a decoration of raspberry sauce on the plate all around the cake, and I said, 'You'd have thought they'd give us a clean plate.' They liked a good laugh."

As we lay side by side, resting in silence, I wondered if John would come home from work and find me there. All her stories could become tedious if it hadn't been for her bubbly animation. Her vibrance kept me in the lightheaded present. She made me forget the meaning of our short lives and put sadness and nostalgia in some other corner of my brain.

"So what do you and John do together?"

"Weekends we might play a round of golf, go bowling, or visit the mall. We get our clothes together at Old Navy and sometimes eat at Chili's or On the Border. Fix the house and cars and walk the dogs. I talk to everyone, but John's quiet—he's embarrassed by me joking with Charlene or Janet or Bobbi."

"Why did you ever come to Tucson when you had that career with the fire department in Dallas?"

"Well, John got this transfer to an engineering job here and thought it was a step up."

"And you?"

"I figured I'd find something. I did sports photography for a while, too, but when I come here, I had no first-responder contacts or nothing. At first, I was excited by all the things they had here like stain glass. They's some entertainment here. You shoulda seen this lady with a monkey last week. We were on the sidewalk, and every time some old fuckers come by on a golf cart, they go past, stop, then back up and say, 'Is that a monkey?' Every single time! So funny! But they's a ton a fuckwads, dipshits, bozos. If they isn't dying, they's close to it. Darlene got cancer now. Woodwork Ronnie got Alzheimer's."

LINDA WANTED ME TO come for the monthly craft fair. "Yeah, babe, this the crap fair; you gotta come."

I would finally meet Bobbi, who apparently enjoyed Linda's merciless humor. She was tall and graceful with a neat perm and a gentle expression. She welcomed me with smiles and an appealing aura of calm. The three of us wandered around all the stalls, and Bobbi made for the boxes of handmade jewelry, where she picked through the rings and necklaces of beads or semiprecious stones. We fluttered though racks of long, multicolored scarves. At the soaps and lotions, we each sniffed at samples. Inside, we lined up for slices of soggy pizza.

The three of us sat outside at a picnic table, and Linda began. "Bobbi, you remember that time when we was having breakfast at the restaurant, and Al and Sue come in?"

"Oh, my goodness, yes!"

"Liz, it was funny. Me and Bobbi watched them. Sue was walking ahead, but Al looked like death. Bobbi says to me, 'A week?' And I laughed. 'Nah, tomorra.'"

Bobbi smiled. I wondered if the macabre comments were because they had both worked in situations involving death. We walked on, and Linda engaged in repartee with buyers and sellers and often had some aside to me about one or other. Eventually, Bobbi said, "Got to go. Glen's expecting me."

We were quiet for a while as we continued our stroll, and I realized Linda's scattershot interactions with her neighbors reflected her wandering brain. Wherever we went, there was a cursory observation, a story, a joke. Even the callous-sounding comments were just passing ideas with no harsh intention beyond making someone laugh.

We came to a big dumpster. "Some a' them old men get stuff outta there. One time, Fred was heaving out a fridge, and he got it to the edge when suddenly it fell on top a him— had ta get the ambulance. There's the restaurant. I was having breakfast with Bobbi when Joe and Ann come in. Joe sits down at the first table as Sue walked on with the waitress. He says, 'I ain't going no further.' So the waitress brought Ann back and gave them menus. Joe says, 'I'll have egg and bacon,' and Ann says to the waitress, 'He ain't getting that.' Then he says, 'Well, French toast then.' And Ann again says, 'He ain't getting that.' Eventually, Joe slams down the menu, and Sue tells the waitress, 'He's getting oatmeal.'"

It wouldn't have been particularly funny if Linda hadn't mimicked the characters so perfectly. She had a talent in that department.

One day when I was at home and out in the desert with Tigger, she called. "Come over to our house, and we can eat with John."

I was taken aback. It was one thing to meet him at a bowling alley or visit the house when he was at work but quite another to be together in their house. John was lounging on the big brown sofa watching TV, his large body lolled back and his feet resting on the coffee table. He had cut his wispy hair and shaved his scruffy beard since I had seen him bowling. He looked almost tidy in his work clothes.

He smiled in welcome. "Lin says you got a kitty. Do you like dogs? Because we got Trooper and Wookie."

We watched Trooper—the old yellow Lab—and Wookie, the little Yorkie, as they played.

"They're great friends," John said as he looked at Trooper. "The big guy is getting old, so it will be hard on Wookie when he dies."

Linda commanded John, "Go get us something at Chick-fil-A." When he left, she said, "He mostly gets our supper." I gathered they typically ate fast food that John picked up after work.

We ate in the very small kitchen. There was just room for two at the tiny, chopping-block table, so John sat up high at a bar separating the kitchen from the living room. He asked about bugs and my house in the Tucson foothills. "You're lucky to have your own pool. There's three here, but they're not close, and we never go near them."

Linda remained quiet.

EVENTUALLY, I WAS PERSUADED to spend a night there. When I arrived, Linda was outside waiting and hugged me as I got out of my car. We went in together.

"Hello, Liz. How's it going?" John asked.

"Fine, thanks, John. And you?"

"Oh, a bit tired. It's been a busy day at work. How's the kitty?"

Nothing was said about my staying the night, so the three of us sat on the big sofa watching the news on TV until John said, "Well, I'll leave it to you two now. I'm off to my room. Goodnight."

After a few such visits, the three of us together felt almost normal.

One Easter, Linda, John, and I were invited to join Bobbi and Glen in their huge, immaculate motor home. Willowy Bobbi, always smiling, was never judgmental about the peculiarity of our situation. Glen cooked. "You like beans, Liz? These frozen ones from Costco are the best. And we got nice ham here from Honey Baked."

We sat in a dining booth that had a good view of a depression in the road outside, and as we ate, we saw a woman riding a bike down and up the other side.

Linda pointed. "Look, Bobbi, it's Charlene. Look at her with her prim little white shorts and ironed blouse. And she got a new perm. Remember how we was riding with her? She got so mad with us for not stopping at a stop sign, and we just laughed and didn't stop at any of them after that."

Bobbi laughed. "Oh, we were bad."

As we ate, I thought how the stories kept the resort visits superficially easy, but Linda needed more than the gossip of a retirement resort. I wanted to expand her world. Meanwhile, she was determined to involve me in her life with John, who appeared very dependent, needing her to make decisions and agreeing to her demands.

The three of us stood around in the garage. John had the hood of his BMW up to clean the engine.

I said, "What a nice car."

"Yeah, got a good deal on it, and it's sweet."

Linda declared, "You gotta do the shocks in my truck."

We left John in the garage and went into the kitchen. "He does the work on my truck. Well, I help him sometimes. But you should see him when we shop at Old Navy. I buy men's clothes, and whatever T-shirt I choose, he gets the exact same one in a big size. It's like he can't think for hisself."

It was later that I really thought about Linda's bossiness and John's silent compliance. Had he become submissive because Linda was bossy, or was he so indolent he had to be pushed? From my glimpses of their life together, it seemed that John spent a large proportion of his time at home on the sofa watching TV. I decided both elements played a part. They had been each other's only real companion for over thirty years and probably took the road that simply worked.

John was always ready to accept me and talk because I was part of Linda's life, and his friendly chatter made it clear that he enjoyed my visits. Yet their home was still their joint home with all Linda's belongings. On one of my later visits, John had put a new, bigger TV in her bedroom. "Get up and fix the electric line in my bedroom," Linda instructed, and he immediately went to the garage to get the tools.

Linda showed me the tiny courtyard of dirt and dead weeds. "It fills up with water in a monsoon storm. Wookie won't go out when it's like that. He pushes the doggie door open just enough and pees right through it."

At the resort, I got to know several of Linda's neighbors. Her main friends tended to be people who were able to engage with her kind of humor, who would talk back or otherwise entertain her. We ran into Bob and Lois when we passed their park model.

"Hi, there. Who's your friend?"

"She's a bug professor."

They laughed. "We need you; we've got crickets in the house!"

Bob called out, "Hey, Linda, do you remember what I taught you in Spanish?"

Linda was silent for once.

"Here it is again then: *el oso cagado en el bosque.*"

"Now I got it," she replied. "*Oso el caca el bosque.* See ya."

We moved on. "This place got so many rules you wouldn't believe. There's this one asshole called Judy. One a' the rules is you gotta always wear a name badge, and when I was forced to, I fixed a badge with 'Trouble' written on it."

FINALLY, I VISITED THE resort on a weekend.

"John, you fix our lunch on the grill." We used a gas grill not far from their house. Linda and I sat on benches and watched John cook.

"How do you like your steak, Liz? Which piece would you like?"

"Medium rare if you can do it."

Linda had her eye on passersby. "Here come Susan and Tom. He was in border patrol, and Susan getting dementia. There goes Judy, and I ain't got my badge! Look at them women coming with a fat little shit-zoo. Never seen them before."

John focused on his job. "Hey, Liz, does this steak look good? Want some of this potato salad? How about some more water?"

We ate with Linda's commentary. "Liz eats it raw. You watch—she has steak with her salt! There goes Charlene on her bike."

Linda wanted me to know John. He seemed pleased that Linda had someone who cared so much about her, and he needed Linda to share me with him to feel he was included. He felt closer to Linda because he knew her lover. The situation was not sustainable, but for the time being, we adapted, and I even became the lubricant in their relationship.

LEAVING THE RESORT AFTER my first day there, I looked across to the prison, where a small dust devil swirled up through the saguaros, and my mind wandered to my childhood in Brisbane. In a strong westerly wind, dust billowed across the eucalyptus forest from cement works upriver. How Mother cursed the white fur that covered everything on those windy days. I saw real dust in the Sahara Desert when I worked on grasshopper migration with Reg. We saw it coming—a distant brown blur. We took down tents as the mass came toward us. We covered the radar dishes that monitored insect night flight and tightly closed the equipment truck. For three hours, we saw nothing but brown as we sat holding hands in a closed Land Rover, listening to eerie whines as the vehicle rocked and thick, sandy dust whipped over us. It was gone by nightfall. Then we watched layers of migrating grasshoppers on an oscilloscope screen. They were detected by radar and flew downwind to where rain was likely.

WHEN I GOT HOME from the resort, I sat gazing at my own dusty shelves, and I drifted off into thinking about dust. In houses, it gets swept up, hosed off porches and cars and paths, shaken from carpets in the garden to send it somewhere else. Landfills have millions of bags of dust from vacuum cleaners. In England, the garbage collector is called the *dustman*. Spray cans of chemicals lift dust onto dusters or stick it to mops. Gallons of water wash dusters and mops. Everything will end up as dust the way mountains erode to plains and energy dissipates as heat. We, too, will become dust, but there will be brilliant sunsets. I cleaned the dust from my house and hosed down the tongues of dust lapping along the edges of the patio, wondering if my relationship with Linda would turn to dust and my own sunset a solitary flash.

8 North Queensland

LINDA BOUNCED INTO THE kitchen with a wide smile, waving a couple of small black sacs with long cords in front of my face.

"Look what I got! They's pockets for us to carry our passports and ID cards in Australia. You put them round your neck. I got one for each of us."

"I'm not wearing that."

Looking at her, I immediately regretted my remark. Linda later brought them out to show my friend Nancy, who smiled. "For the beginner traveler." Seeing Linda's deflation, she continued, "They're good though, especially for older people." Linda stuffed them in a drawer under all her old sweaters. "You look after the important papers," she said softly, giving me her passport.

She began checking airlines and timetables for our trip. From the computer, her rather small face looked up at me with open mouth when she discovered Seat Guru.

"Here's where we find the best seats on *every* kind of plane!"

I let her make all the choices. I was eager to revisit my first home, so desperately loved in my youth, but most of all I was enthusiastic for Linda. I loved her fervor. She took special charge of luggage. "You can't take them ancient suit-cases; they's covered in scratches and patches."

She didn't understand my attachment to forty-year-old Samsonite cases that needed straps and were covered with old, stained shipping labels for Southampton, New Delhi, and Lagos. "You gotta get new ones with wheels." She made rainbow-colored name tags to attach outside and typed our names and addresses on cards to put inside.

She researched possibilities on the internet. "Babe, gotta do the Great Barrier Reef and see Sydney and all the coast, and I wanna hold a koala!"

Before the big day—September 13, 2006—Linda splashed around in my swimming pool as she learned to snorkel. She kept her Palm Pilot, iPod Nano, headphones, re-laxation tapes, and anti-anxiety pills ready in brand-new hand luggage.

"You need to take a good book to read," I said.

"Oh, yes, babe, I's a carnivorous reader."

We slept at the resort the night beforehand, and John drove us to the airport. He seemed happy for Linda, but as he drove off, he called to me with a grin. "Glad it's you and not me getting on that plane."

He knew Linda was nervous, but I felt that the open impli-cation that Linda was not up to the moment was not the way to defeat unease. We would show him! Through security and into the waiting lounge, Linda was her usual self. "Look at that woman reading with the page an inch from her nose. Look at that girl; she has an electric outlet for her laptop. Look how ugly, how old, how thin, looks like a bum, see them two talking to each other across the room on fucking cell phones." Then a tall man in a dark suit and silk cravat nearly tripped over our feet. He stopped to apologize in an unfamiliar foreign accent. One of those passport pockets dangled from his neck!

"Beginner," Linda whispered to me with glee.

But we both knew that panic might be around the corner, and I went to the desk to explain, "My companion is severely claustrophobic, and we need a preboarding pass."

We were first onto the plane and sat in the two front seats. "I feel great, babe," she announced as she photographed all the planes in sight from the window while we taxied to the runway. An hour later, we were in the brown air of Los Angeles and on to a hotel for the night.

The flight over the Pacific the next day was the real test, but Linda discovered another Texan behind us, and the two of them chatted for hours while I watched movies and dozed. At the airport hotel in Sydney that night, Linda was ecstatic.

"Babe, the flight was great, and I got you all to myself for a whole *seven* weeks."

I smiled. "And I have you." We had never been together for so long, let alone in a foreign country, and I fleetingly thought, *Seven weeks!*

Next morning was another novelty for her—a train ride. We took the train to Central Station and then changed to the North Shore line, and in an hour we met Steve, one of my former graduate students, now a professor at Sydney University. His spacious family home at Wahroonga was surrounded by eucalyptus trees busy with restless rainbow lorikeets, squawking sulfur-crested cockatoos, kookaburras, and brown cuckoo doves. Steve, still fresh-faced and warmly welcoming, fed us with buttery-tasting barramundi he had caught himself. He seemed little changed from the ever-happy student of our English days when he spent weekends trout fishing. We ate outdoors with his English wife, Lesley, and their two young boys, who were sharing secret jokes.

As the conversation turned to research, Steve and I sat talking as Lesley cleared the dishes, the boys disappeared, and

Linda played with their spaniel. But it was hard to focus on science with my head full of the sight of gray-green foliage and the aromatic smell of my eucalyptus past.

Back in the city center at the Isis hotel, our room was just big enough for the bed. We wandered around the iconic opera house, and Linda remarked on the "sails" as she got her hundreds of photographs. We took one of the old green-and-cream ferries over the sparkling harbor, busy with sailing boats, to Manly Ocean beach, and I was delighted to see that it still had the long row of Norfolk Island pines where we'd picnicked when I was very young. The Botanic Gardens with views of the harbor was another memory jolt: Grandpa walking me as a small child around the garden headland to Mrs. Macquarie's Chair, a bench hand-carved in 1810 by convicts in the sandstone cliffs for the wife of Governor Macquarie. The bench had a view of all the boats streaming in and out of Circular Quay.

"HEY, BABE, THEY'S ALL sulfur-crested cockatoos on the grass! And giant bats up the trees!"

"Yes, those are the flying foxes we used to get in our Brisbane garden when I was a kid."

We spent a morning at the two-hundred-year-old Hyde Park Barracks, from Sydney's earliest days. It was designed by convict architect Francis Greenway, who'd received a fourteen-year sentence in England for forgery. The old barracks is now a museum about early colonial Australia, and Linda tested out one of the hammocks: "Look, I's a sleeping convict." At the State Library of New South Wales—the oldest library in Australia—we saw James Cook's first map of the Southern Hemisphere. Copperplate engraved and yellowed in places, it showed Tasmania still joined to the mainland. I was proud to be showing Linda my long-ago home country, but she was most fascinated by the places she had seen in movies or on the internet. She jumped up and down at Circular Quay when she spotted the liner *The World* in dock.

"Babe, it's the largest private residential ship in the world! Rich people live in luxury and vote for which exotic places they should visit."

As Linda rattled on, my thoughts were not on *The World* but rather on *SS Canberra*, the P&O liner berthed in the same place, which took me to Europe when I was twenty-two. So long ago, I made my way up the gangplank onto the sleek new ship incongruously nestled among city buildings and from a high deck threw red and blue paper streamers down to friends and all the other little people standing on the wharf below until a tugboat pulled us away, and all the streamers tore apart and fluttered in the breeze.

On the plane to Cairns in North Queensland a few days later, we sat in what became our typical three-seat configuration. We wanted to sit next to one another, but Linda wanted an aisle seat. She leaned across me to offer a Hershey bar to the middle-aged woman in a floral muumuu by the window.

"Ta, love," the woman said.

In her turn, the woman offered us candy. "Want a lolly? You gotta get Tim Tams in Cairns—best fings ever. Get only original though, not them new varieties."

Sitting back, I shut my eyes and let them talk Tim Tams, some kind of chocolate cookie.

The Club Crocodile Hotel in the heart of Cairns was built in 1885 with wide colonial verandahs. Refurbished in 1967, it was rather dark and lacked comfortable beds, but I liked the faded charm. It had what even the simplest Australian hotels have—a tiny fridge with fresh milk for the all-important early-morning tea. That first evening, we walked to the bustling night market with tropical fruit stalls, line-ups of long Indian skirts, trays of opals, secondhand books, snorkels, ice cream, and foods from every country. We bought fried rice for supper, and I left Linda to get a chair massage while I wandered back to the hotel. I was happy to have a little time alone to let the heavy, sweet odors of tropical flowers and ripe mangos in the humid night take me back to my Queensland childhood. Later, Linda appeared in our room crying.

"What happened?"

She brought out a little blue notebook and wrote, "GOT LOST." She had never done such a thing before, and I felt her stiff in my embrace, but slowly my apprehensive sweetheart, normally so confidently full of life, relaxed. "Don't know directions in the Southern Hemisphere."

At our first snorkel, I held her hand as we drifted in the clear-blue Coral Sea at Fitzroy Island and was thrilled at her total and unusual absorption, never even looking toward me. On our return, tired and hungry, she was down in the mouth: "I got a tummy take." Would she cope with travel in North Queensland? Would she adapt to all the new places and be satisfied with a potential lack of comfort? I was faintly nervous, but she was in high spirits the next day as we explored Cairns.

"Oh, look, babe; they's made a swimming pool by the beach that's bigger than three football fields." The Esplanade Lagoon sported five huge poles that rose high out of the blue-green expanse of the lagoon, topped with massive woven-steel fish sculptures that seemed to be swimming in blue sky with a background of ultramarine sea.

"Wow, great art, babe. And, look, Aboriginal people and so many pelicans. All those birds with curvy beaks at the bottle brush flowers—some red and some blue. Love the huge water park with all the little kids!"

We rented a car, and Linda drove us north beside palm-tree-lined Cairns beaches, the calm water protected by the outer reef. Sitting on the grass at almost-empty Trinity Beach, looking at the so-blue sea, we gobbled down salty fish and chips from paper wrappers.

"Fuck!"

I looked to see Linda frowning and followed her eyes to a black and yellow warning notice: "Marine Stingers." And a picture of a stick figure with tentacles of a jellyfish around his legs. "Box jellyfish—not a worry in spring," I assured her.

We ended up at lonely Wonga Beach and checked into Daintree Palms Beach Resort. It was a bit deserted and the garden unkempt. Dated and rundown, it would have been considered smart in my childhood, with its little lake, fountains, and its own unpretentious café. The office was tiny and devoid of decoration or any kind of information, but our little room had louvers looking out to coconut palms and spreading poinciana trees covered in red flowers with white flag petals. There were no phones, nightstands, or curtains. Linda was uncharacteristically quiet as her eyes went around the simple room. She tested the louvers: "No insect screens, Jesus."

"Let's go to the beach," I said, hoping to alleviate her misgivings.

We found a narrow path through palm trees full of screeching rainbow lorikeets to walk on the long, empty beach. Linda looked back at where we had emerged from the palms, frowning.

"What if we can't find where we get back to our place?"

She built a pile of driftwood and drew a big arrow in the sand but couldn't relax until we were back at the resort.

"There's a huge gap under our door. Something might get in."

I lay on the hard bed with thin pillows, thinking of a simple beach house at Caloundra north of Brisbane, where I'd stayed as a child with family friends. Sand blew in under the door as I lay on a little cot by an open window and listened to the sound of surf crashing on the beach. I needed time to enjoy my sentimental musings that took me back to a much-loved vacation.

"You shower first."

Linda turned the water on, and in no time the door opened and a voice commanded, "Get your ass in here."

"Why?"

"Get your ass here."

I got up slowly and shuffled to the bathroom, where Linda, hand on hip, glared at the round light fitting. "Look! It screamed at me!"

"Ah, lovely, a little brown gecko."

"What's it going to do to me?"

"Nothing. It's harmless."

"It's going to bite me in the night."

"No worries."

She had her shower, keeping a wary eye on the gecko inside the globe.

When it was my turn, she called, "Keep watching." At intervals, she put her head around the door to see. "Oh, god."

In the night, the gecko made *chak-chak* noises. "Did you hear that?" But by morning, it was nowhere to be found.

"Must have went out through that big-ass gap under the door. In Los Angeles, we had a luxury hotel with big pool, spa, and steam room. And the Holiday Inn at Sydney airport was quite fancy. Then that cheap Isis hotel in a sleazy area of central Sydney, the budget Club Crocodile in Cairns, and now only a cheap-ass old-fashion dump. Babe, it's been a long decline."

I smiled. I loved the place and knew that she wasn't so much criticizing as worrying. What new things were there to be fearful of? How primitive would this foreign country be? I put my arms around her.

Driving on north through dense dripping rainforest, we took the ferry across the Daintree River. It held just a couple of cars and swung sideways in the strong current as Linda held tight to the steering wheel of the car. Over the mountains to Cape Tribulation, we passed notices about watching out for the massive cassowary birds. The shy flightless bird, taller than most people, peered out of the forest, its bright blue neck with a floppy red wattle and a head topped with a tall, pointed helmet. "There it is, babe, a huge Cassandra."

We sped past yellow warning signs about the dangers of crocodiles. "Don't want to get crocolated, eh?"

The five-star Ferntree resort that Steve had recommended delighted us with boardwalks through the rain forest, a walk-in pool, and an outdoor restaurant set in a grove of kauri trees, those remnants of an ancient flora shared now with New Zealand and Chile—countries conjoined two hundred million years ago. Our room was lined on one side with dark hardwood cabinets. Opposite, a wall of glass looked into dense forest. Steps led up to a bedroom with a king-size bed. Then more steps up to a balcony overlooking the pool and white flowers of lilies and ginger. Linda's eyes opened very wide. "This the real thing, babe!"

We walked through the tiny village to a deserted bay. Steep, cloud-topped mountains ran down to the beach edged with cream-flowered sea hibiscus trees.

Linda stared out at the bay. "Babe, no pier—how's we getting out to the reef tomorrow?"

Back at the resort, we watched from the top floor as the sun slipped below the trees. Evening descended quickly, and dozens of fruit bats took off. Suddenly, Linda jumped up. "What the fuck is that grunting noise?" And then we saw it—a scrub turkey messing about in the undergrowth.

"Oh, babe, we's living right in the forest!"

"Yes, watch that big black bird with its red neck and head. They scratch up the leaf litter into mounds and put their eggs in the middle to keep warm. But I think it's just searching for food."

The snorkeling trip the next day was an exploration at the outer reef. I am the stronger swimmer and don't even care for fins, so I held Linda's hand tightly. We drifted together in the water, gazing through goggles at so much color, oblivious of everything above in the warm tropical air. Linda took photos of the dazzling fish—big blue-and-pink parrot fish, flat yellow butterfly fish that held station over a rock encrusted with pink algae that looked like bubblegum, orange fish with black fins, schools of scarlet or iridescent blue midgets darting in and out of corals and sponges, and a thousand others. Corals were more delicate with pinks and white, pale blues and cream. Tube worms encased in calcium extended flowery whorls of royal blue, magenta, or gold tentacles that retracted when we touched them. Linda watched me touch the bright-blue mantle of a giant clam, making it snap shut, and I saw her eyes smile behind her goggles when she found a pink-and-purple one and touched it herself.

Hours later, heading back to land, we watched streams of white foam and a deep wake through the choppy, dark-blue water. Linda, smiling with an open mouth, ended up with, "So much color all at once! We been snorkeling twice, babe. It was amazing."

The sight of all the fish and corals swept through my head as I remembered the joy of marine biology on Heron Island farther south in the glory days of the Great Barrier Reef. Our professor declared that fishing every day was a professorial perquisite, and that pleased the rest of us because we were free to snorkel all day, and he brought us fresh fish for supper. Years later, I took Reg to Heron Island to relive those heady student days with him. He was not a swimmer, but we paddled out over the fringing reef at low tide, bending over all the corals, giant clams, sea urchins, star fish, and those tube worms with tentacles like tiny red or blue feather dusters. Our time was so immersed in the fine details of marine creatures and their modes of life that we never considered photos. How sunburnt we got as we forgot time! It was different with Linda. The visual splendor took over our senses, and biology came second.

From Cape Trib, we headed south again to Port Douglas and the Wildlife Habitat. Once again, Linda was bright-eyed spotting all the native marsupials, from kangaroos and wallabies to spotted quolls and striped possums. It was the tiny feathertail glider that fascinated her most, though, with its silky gray-brown fur and big dark eyes.

"Could sit on my finger," she marveled, smiling with eyebrows raised.

We stopped at a seafood store, where Linda spied Morton Bay bugs. Her eyes widened at the sight of these local lobsters. "Gotta try those." I bought an Aussie meat pie that came with a memory of university classes and hurried lunches.

In the tiny courtyard of our hotel, Linda wolfed down the bugs. "They's fucking amazing," she declared as she looked at me, her face and spread hands covered in scraps of lobster meat.

The snorkeling trip from Port Douglas was rough, and Linda was mortally afraid of being seasick. We slithered carefully down from the boat, me in long-sleeved pajamas against sunburn and clutching a floatation noodle and Linda clasping me. Her worried face showed through her goggles in the choppy water, but she got her photos all the same.

That evening, we were both very tired after a day in rough water, and Linda said, "I feel so adjicated. Our room's too small; there's no bathtub, no nightstand."

"Stop moaning," I replied sharply and began my diary of the day.

I hadn't got far when she handed me a bookmark from the Wildlife Habitat with a Ulysses butterfly picture on it. On the back side, she had written in her usual capital letters, "I love you so much, babe. This is for you to bookmark and remember all our great adventures. All my love forever from your bublet." I kissed her tenderly.

Holding her on the bed, it dawned on me that Linda's eruptions of complaint were not just childish grumbles. They were indicators of something deeper. There had been such an avalanche of anxieties: driving on the "wrong" side of the road, accents and slang she couldn't decipher, no mental map of new places, and all the potential new dangers and discomforts she couldn't control. I had never been much afraid of anything and had been very fortunate in my varied life, leaving me slow to realize that Linda, brought up under the suffocating protection of older parents and then John, had never known a wider world. Underneath her excitement about the newness of Australia was a very deep well of apprehension. But I was confident that Australia was opening doors for her.

At Pandanus Beach Campground the next night, we sizzled some lamb chops on an Aussie BBQ—a gas fire under a metal plate with a grease drain in the middle. We were surrounded by eucalyptus, coconut palms, pandanus, and other rainforest trees with epiphytes like bird's nest ferns attached.

We held hands watching flocks of green fig birds with red rings around their eyes as they tackled dark-red umbrella-tree fruits, friar birds dipping their black heads into banksia flowers noisily slurping nectar, and multicolored rainbow lorikeets tearing at hibiscus flowers.

"Where next, babe?"

"We must visit a mountain village and the World Heritage rainforest west of Cairns. Koalas!" A deep-green forest drive took us up to Kuranda. First was the Butterfly Sanctuary, which was a world of color. Green and yellow birdwings, iridescent blue morphos, and dozens of other butterfly species flitted and landed or swept across the whole mass of orchids and ferns and bromeliads, while memories of my childhood love of butterflies returned with a passion. In Bird World, there were hundreds of species, mostly parrots. Red-and-green king parrots, pink-and-gray galahs, lime-green eclectus parrots, rainbow lorikeets—all littering the bushes like enormous Christmas decorations and shrieking as they flew from tree to tree. Linda and John had pet parrots, so this place held special interest as she searched for species she knew. Some can be purchased in the United States, and she wondered, "So many different kinds. They's hundreds of thousands of dollars flying around!" But when we saw a tawny frogmouth, we both laughed. Related to nightjars, it stood motionless, beak pointing up, with its classic expression of misery. For weeks afterward, Linda would put on her best tawny frogmouth expression and ask, "What am I?"

Finally, we got to the Koala Garden. "So soft," Linda crooned, smiling and looking at me with those flashing dark eyes and then looking gently down at her favorite Australian animal.

"Look at me holding her. Look at her. Oh, babe, I love this little girl."

I took in the picture of my sweetheart—small build, shapely brown legs, brand-new knee-length shorts, T-shirt with the Australian flag, and no bra. Her black hair in a crew-cut above a little round face absorbed with the sleepy koala as she kept slowly stroking the very thick fur. We each got the ritual photos holding a koala.

"So soft," she kept repeating as she touched the furry round ears. "Look at me holding her. Look at her."

That evening as we were drifting off to sleep, she whispered, "I love that koala." At intervals during the rest of the trip, she opened her book where she had secreted the photo of herself holding a koala. Years later, she kept a small copy in her wallet to whip out and show friends and neighbors.

I loved seeing Linda with her surprised face and her smile of delight at so many things Australian. And I loved the unexpected silences as she took in something that was new to her and then looked at me with raised eyebrows as if to say "Do you love it too?" Of course I did, but I was twenty-two when I abandoned my beloved country. I stood with my parents at South Brisbane train station. They didn't come to Sydney, where I would board the ship. Our electric goodbyes rose through the shafts of smoke, lost in the hiss of steam, the bang and clatter of buffers, and the anticipation of excitement ahead.

My mother said, "I know you will come back, darling; you so love the bush."

"Oh, yes," I had replied, though moisture was gathering on her upper lip, and her knuckles were white on her old leather bag—things I only remembered later from the ashes of that summer afternoon. At the time, I was impatient for the shrill whistle and slamming doors: the beginning of adventure.

I didn't visit Australia for seven years, when my adored

mother was dying, but the sight and smell of eucalyptus trees all over the world had often made me homesick. Now, my parents long gone and beloved husband dead too, I was back in my first home with a Texan sweetheart. How simple and good it was, traveling together, not thinking about what lay ahead, just basking in the happy present with intermittent nostalgic memories.

As we drove south, passing cane fields and banana plantations with patches of so-green rainforest, I looked up at the mountains of the Great Divide to the west, the highest ones hidden in clouds until we got to Mission Beach. The doors of the cabin there were inches off the floor, and the bathroom featured a stainless-steel sink and toilet.

"Oh, babe, it's like prison. Animals gonna get in, sand in the bed."

But outside, she got her first sight of wild kangaroos hopping across clearings in the bush and called in excitement. "There they are, babe, wild ones. Look at them; they's hopping, hopping. Look at them, look at them! Oh, this is what I wanted to see! Australia!"

Dark-green rainforest mountains gave way to gray-greens as we continued south. In our silences, it was such eucalyptus forests that absorbed me—memories of teenage years when I sat against white peeling trunks to write my sentimental poems. The crinkle of brittle fallen leaves and the uniquely clean pungent smell in the air would become a poem in my head.

As we approached the town of Ayr, I remembered 1960. "In student days, I spent a summer near here, stringing tobacco leaves with other women in a barn."

"Stringing?"

"You take leaves in bunches of three and tie them up all along a thin pole, and the poles are hung in a shed for curing.

When I hitchhiked through here, the campground was full of rough-sounding boys, so I asked at the police station if I could camp under the mango tree in their yard. The cop said, 'Darlin', I'll give you a cell.'" He even brought a cup of tea to the cell in the morning."

"You Aussies are crazy."

Sailing from Airlie Beach among the Whitsunday Islands was an adrenaline rush—dazzling with the famous brilliance of azure blues and snow-white sands. There were just twelve of us on the boat together with the skipper. For a time, Linda took the tiller, allowing me to get the photo she wanted of herself with a background of shimmering blue. A good breeze, the sound of water and wind, and nothing else in this blue-and-white space took our breath away.

"Oh, babe, it's so cool. I could do this forever."

At the tiny historic cane-cutter's cottage where we stayed, we sat on the verandah talking about the sailing trip we had so enjoyed while we watched wallabies gently hopping about and grazing. Then we walked out among them. Small bundles of leaves hung from young trees, and Linda stretched up for one.

"Fuck, babe!" she screamed as a multitude of yellowish-brown ants descended on her.

"Oh, bub, they are weaver ants that make nests by knitting the leaves together with silk from their larvae."

"Are they going to sting me?"

"Well, they can bite, and they have a kind of acid spray."

Linda flailed her arms. "Fuck."

"No worries."

North Queensland was almost over. Lying awake to the sound of Linda breathing deeply, I thought of all we had seen throughout four hundred miles of driving and weeks of adventure. Linda had reveled in it. Koalas more than lived up to expectation. But it had been a different Linda from the one on our motor home trips, where she was the one in charge. Apart from a few changed or invented words, there'd been no parade of clever nonsense verbiage. There had been a lot of silence. Her brain was busy with the total newness of her first foreign vacation, and I sensed the timorousness, uncertainty, and anxiety. Perhaps more importantly, her confidence was undercut by not being in control—so much was new, and she had ceded the decision-making to me. I wondered if there would be a long-term effect.

9 Relatives

LINDA DROVE US FROM Brisbane airport to my sister's house in the very leafy suburb of Chapel Hill, and I saw her waiting outside the front door. I ran across the front lawn, and we both called, "My sweet little sister" while flinging our arms around each other. Jennifer was the tiny little sister, and I was the much younger little sister. The diminutive seventy-year-old with short gray hair still radiated classic good looks. Her pants had little pockets up the sides of the legs— she bought her clothes at a children's store.

"So this is Linda. Hello and welcome. How was the trip? Did you have fun? Lovely to see you both." Her black-and-brown rescue dog, Whoopie, ran around us in circles.

Like many houses in hilly Brisbane Queensland, hers was built on a steep slope. We walked inside to the open living and dining rooms, and from the adjacent kitchen, stairs took us down to a lower level at the back. Jennifer showed us a small room with a cupboard, a bookcase, and a framed photograph of our grandfather. A window looked out to a silky oak tree covered in enormous, long broom heads of golden flowers, and a door opened onto the back lawn. There was a mattress on either side of the room.

I kissed her on the cheek. "That's fine for us."

Linda's mouth fell open as Jennifer explained, "I don't know what you people do."

Weeks later, I repeatedly heard "Jennifer so tarny, and mattresses on either side of the room!"

SOFT-SPOKEN JENNIFER WAS WIDE-EYED with astonishment at Linda's loud voice and Texas accent as we sat at the kitchen table: "We kept doing snorkels in North Queensland. It was unbelievable, and we held koalas and went sailing and ate Moreton Bay bugs." My sister's attention, though, was mostly on me, and as our eyes met, we smiled our affection. She and I were the last ones left—our parents and both brothers long dead. I'd never known her well. She'd left home to go nursing when I was eleven, then worked and married in England, and after I left Australia, she returned with her young Dutch family. We'd lived on opposite sides of the world most of our lives.

Leonora, Jennifer's elder daughter, made a rushed visit with eleven-year-old Alastair, whose father was Thai, and eight-year-old Loani, whose father was Turkish. They all listened with astonishment to Linda's "How y'all doing? Y'all so different from Liz." But Leonora was in a somewhat manic state, with her startling green eyes, wild curly hair, and waving arms. "Love you. Had to just come and welcome you," as she embraced me with a frenetic hug before dragging the kids off for Alastair's football practice.

Linda had a rapt audience in Jennifer. "We stayed in these places that didn't have screens, and we had lizards and everything in the bathroom." As she rattled on, my own memories flooded back—standing at ten beside my sixteen-year-old sister when she played "Pedro the Fisherman" on the piano as Mother sang along, watching her beautiful heart-shaped face at the mirror as she sat trimming her eyebrows with tweezers and talked about falling in love with Peter or Bruce. There was that strapless red ball gown she'd made that Mother objected to, and there were hems to change to suit current fashions. She had been the sweet feminine one with a musical laugh and lots of boyfriends and was our father's favorite.

"Bub, my sister was a nurse. She cared for me when I was seven with mumps and then measles."

Later, I would explain to her how Jennifer had spent years caring for our mother and then her beloved husband, Herman, each of them dying from cancer at home.

In the morning, the three of us had breakfast on the upper-level back verandah looking out at the native trees—tall eucalyptus, bushy lilly pilly with pink berries, and a dense tuckeroo tree where olive-green fig birds squabbled for the cream-colored fruit. Haunting, fluty songs of pied currawongs and butcher birds filled the air and turned all the other birdsong into chatter. I remembered Mother's jewel-green eyes piercing mine long ago when a currawong was singing: "Listen, darling! You will never forget the song, will you?"

"Holy fuck. Smoke!" Linda exclaimed as Jennifer deliberately burned her toast black.

Jennifer laughed. "I had to get a power outlet out here because I kept setting off the smoke alarm in the kitchen."

She covered the charcoal with butter and Vegemite as an incredulous Linda watched. "What's that black stuff? Looks like axle grease."

"Linda, you should try it. We all love it."

"No way, hozay."

Looking down to the lawn with washing hanging on the line, I admired the garden with yellow banksias, scarlet bottle brush, buddleia flowers covered in butterflies, and assorted daisies. "Wow, little sister, you've become a gardener."

"I took to plants when the girls left home. Oh, look down by the pool at the bottom of the garden." And we saw a scrub turkey arranging piles of leaf litter in the shade of an umbrella tree.

Jennifer jumped up. "Forgot something," she said and rushed inside. She brought out chunks of ground beef and laid them on the railing. In less than a minute, two kookaburras landed. One took the meat to eat in a eucalyptus tree; the other bolted down a piece on the railing and then began the famous loud chuckle followed by raucous cackling, making Linda gaze with an open mouth. "They really do laugh!"

Linda was fascinated by family. She often looked at Jennifer and me to find similarities.

"I don't look like any a' the half-sisters and brothers I's seen photos of. I thought full siblings would look more like each other." And so began the story of her birth mother and the twenty children she had borne and sold. Jennifer was spellbound and probably horrified, though she gave no sign. Meanwhile, Linda was studying us both. "I can tell you's sisters but not sure exactly why."

AT LONE PINE KOALA Sanctuary, dozens of large enclosures were scattered among the eucalyptus trees; one was for visitors to hold the koalas. When Linda was given one with especially furry ears, "I think it's a boy; it stinks."

But she cradled it fondly in one arm for the necessary photo. Then we found the nursery enclosure, and as we watched, a tiny koala emerged from its mother's pouch and crawled onto her back.

"Babe, *look* at that little one on its mommy. How I love them!"

We were, of course, smitten—it could have been a poster for Australian tourism.

We watched the slow-moving koala with its piggyback baby for at least an hour as Linda exclaimed at every little move, but eventually we went on to watch other koalas: half-grown kids, old ones, pregnant mothers, elderly. Most of them were sound asleep. At a high lookout, we could see across the Brisbane River to where I'd spent my teenage years and rowed my little pram dinghy on this brown river winding through eucalyptus forest, floating alone and imagining my dream cabin among the trees. If the tide was strong and a barge came by, the helmsman would call, "Want a tow?" and I would take the rope. I'd often rowed across to this koala haven.

Linda put her arm around me. "You sad, babe?"

"A strange kind of sadness but happy too, bub. This was my home place."

"I love to be with you in your first home place."

I took Leonora, Alastair and Loani, and my old friend Jill to stay on Stradbroke Island, which forms part of the outer barrier to Moreton Bay and the Brisbane River estuary. We wandered the headland on the ocean side—gorges wild with foam and spray—and then along empty white-sand surf beaches. Willowy Jill was a source of wonder to Linda and my family with her erudite expressions ("How you hurtle your way through the challenge of survival"), never mind her cascading clothes and hat with a two-foot brim. The two of us reminisced about our time as students at University of Queensland and later as roommates in London.

"Remember the dirty brown bedsit room with cracked windows in Camden Town? We shared a bathroom with two old women on the floor above, where we put pennies in a gas heater to get hot water. Those mad women kept stealing the bath plug."

She had returned to Australia, a widow with four-year-old twins, while Reg and I eventually went to California, but over the years and distance, we remained close.

The kids had boogie boards for the surf, but Jill and I just floundered about in the waves while Linda took photos—me coming out of a wave with legs in the air, Jill standing with arms folded over droopy suit, elastic long gone.

Linda searched for anything unusual on the beach. "Look, inflatable rescue boat; look, shark head; nice kayak with painted birds."

"You see everything," Jill said.

"I's a idiot savant—well, without the savant." And Jill doubled over with laughter.

Back at Jennifer's place, the three of us walked the treelined streets and hillsides blue with blossom-covered jac-aranda trees. In my youth, the violet-blue color always meant study week and the coming exams at the end of the school year. As Linda played with Whoopie and talked to neighbors, I went back to that youthful time when I held my breath running through the trees and laughing as the breezes blew through my hair.

Jennifer and I visited the house of our young lives. Friendly owners let us roam, but there was no sign of our mother's luxuriant gardens, and wilderness replaced all Father's fruit trees. At the front of the house, I didn't try the rotten stairs to the veranda, but the past swam before my eyes. I sat on those stairs with my parents on teenage evenings as they drank Beenleigh rum and smoked Craven A cigarettes while a mosquito coil burned beside us. The persistent sound of crickets irritated Mother and lowered her threshold for combat as she geared for her exasperation with the man who looked to the distance with vacant violet eyes. He was listening for something he could comprehend as the squall of her anger, impatient with silence masquerading as wisdom, gathered its daily strength. The sun dropped behind ghost gums along the riverside, greens faded to gray, ribbons of stringy bark darkened on moon-pale trunks, and whip birds called in the underbrush. Night enveloped us.

LINDA ENJOYED RAVING ABOUT koalas and getting to know my family. She got a kick out of shocking them and making them laugh. Jennifer's younger daughter, gentle Christina, arrived from Canberra with Nick and Sophie—two charmers aged eight and ten. One evening, Leonora came also with her young children, Alastair and Loani, and Jennifer organized a formal dinner for the nine of us. Linda had never seen so much cutlery, glasses, and condiments. But she was in her element with the four kids. At dinner, she picked out two asparagus spears and hung one from either side of her mouth: "Look, walrus."

All the children gasped and looked at Jennifer to see if she was shocked before daring to laugh. But Linda was a hit all round with her ready wit and loud laughter at everything and everybody. She was able to dissipate family conflicts. During our time in Brisbane, I developed a new fondness for my little sister.

SOUTHWARD AGAIN THROUGH ENDLESS eucalyptus forests and then the white surf beaches of the Gold Coast. I remembered family day trips to the beach in our old black 1952 Standard Vanguard when we had to make stops because the radiator overheated and the dreadful day when my rare bottle of lemonade was used to cool it. Then days of lying face up in the sun on the beach for hours with teenage friends with the booming sound of waves before we knew about skin cancer.

From our cabin at Byron Bay, Linda and I walked the great semicircle of white sand and ate fish and chips in a howling wind among a sprinkling of hippie youth lying flat out in the sun, just as I had done decades earlier. We paddled where waves rushed up over damp sand and then slid slowly back, leaving delicate jellyfish and bright-blue Portuguese men-of-war with their trailing stingers.

"No fucking sea glass."

"You don't need sea glass." They meant more to her than the wondrous cockleshells and cowries that I had collected along the surf line or in rock pools long ago.

From the old lighthouse on the headland, we hiked a banksia-lined path beside high cliffs out to the end of Cape Byron, the most easterly point of mainland Australia. We didn't see the whales that migrate past, but a long surfing beach stretched south into the distance, and extending north, a string of white sandy scallops faced the deep-blue Pacific.

We were exhilarated from the hike, wind, and expansive views, but as I thought of the decades that separated me from long-ago beach scenes, I felt somber. I had abandoned a beautiful country.

"Your amazing country, babe."

"So strange how coming back makes me remember things I thought I had forgotten."

On the beach at Coffs Harbour, we encountered a couple wearing Yellowstone T-shirts.

"You from the States?" Linda asked eagerly.

"Sure. Our boat's being repaired here, so we're stuck for a while."

"Do you know Al and Debbie—they was sailing across to here from California?"

"Of course. What a surprise to meet someone who knows them!"

It *was* a surprise. Al and Debbie, friends from Tucson, often talked about their trip across the Pacific and the sailing fraternity they interacted with en route.

Linda talked on as I looked vacantly to the ocean. Then she breathlessly wrote down their names to tell Al and Debbie later. "Such a co-inkidink."

WE FOUND FOREST RANCH in the little inland township of Bulahdelah in midafternoon. It promised the horse rides I had told her would be part of our trip. The property was at the end of a dirt road with grassy slopes and lily ponds, surrounded by eucalyptus forest and weeping myall trees. We were the only guests, but we did spend time trying to escape the ten-year-old daughter of the owners, who followed us everywhere.

Linda grumbled, "Chaps my ass—they don't trim the horses' hooves" as we rode through the mixed eucalyptus and paper-bark trees, with dark-green rainforest in the gullies, and saw wallabies and goannas. "Fuck, look at that huge lizard thang." Hidden whip birds called through the forest. "What's that?" And then we saw one—olive green with black head and crest as it pecked in the leaf litter.

In bed late the next morning, Linda said, "You wouldn't be lazing like this at home."

I was learning from Linda to just let things go and let each day and hour look after itself. I bent to her dislike of planning. Let's wait and see, decide later, see how I feel. It was a new experience for me, and I liked it. After a life of timetables and lists and never enough time, I had finally relaxed. I pulled Linda onto the bed and ran my hand through her short hair. "All your fault."

EVENTUALLY WE WERE READY for Canberra and time with Christina's family.

"I just loves meeting your family. I got no family, and I get to know yours so I can know you more."

"I know your adoptive dad had no family, but what happened to all your Cajun mom's relatives? You had fun with some of them, and you told me about an uncle that took you fishing."

"When Mom died, they disowned me. Them Cajuns are into blood relatives."

In the ensuing silence, I thought about what it means to have a lot of genetic relatives. I had never considered that it might be so important. Most of mine were strangers after my life of more than forty years oceans away.

The first evening in Canberra, we reunited with Christina. As she made pasta, she wanted to know all about our trip since we'd seen her in Brisbane. She had an alluring pixie face and short blond hair specially brushed every which way. I just wanted to watch her.

"Did you visit the Blue Mountains?"

"Oh, yes," Linda chimed in as she looked around the kitchen, hoping the food would not be too fancy. "It was good, and we stayed in a hotel that's really old."

"Did you see the Three Sisters?"

"Nah. Thick fog. But I got great shots of Japanese tourists standing in front of where them big rock things were supposed to be. So funny."

Christina chuckled. Her Italian husband, Domenic, hovered over her at the stove, making sure she was cooking in the way he liked it. Sophie and Nick, who had been fascinated by Linda in Brisbane, laughed constantly while they played poker with her at the dining-room table.

Finally, the table was set with candles for the Italian meal. Domenic gave us a bit of a sermon on local politics and Aboriginal affairs. We told them all about our travels, with Linda adding extra anecdotes. "You shoulda seen all the parrots in Kuranda—worth a fortune. You shoulda seen Liz snorkeling in jammies. She was always the last one to get back in the boat."

When we were alone, Linda exclaimed, "Sophie does look like Christina, but it's amazing how most people in your family don't look like each other at all, and they's all very different kinds of people. Strange."

"It's normal really. My brothers didn't look a bit like me. It's not just what characteristics get inherited but what happens with the mix. Genes affect each other."

Our initial visit in Canberra was to the Australian War Memorial. It was Linda's first experience of imposing federal buildings and museums. "Big-ass building, eh? These make-up scenes are amazing," she said of all the dioramas.

My grandfathers, father, and uncles served in the world wars, but my father had refused to talk about his time in service, so I was keen to see the records. I discovered that he enlisted in the Air Force in 1942 when I was just one year old, soon after the Japanese attack on Darwin and the bombing at Pearl Harbor. He spent time in Darwin and in the Philippines, but I found no mention of active service.

Jennifer said our father had been quite interactive before the war, and my mother told us that he'd made the fancy beaded belts hanging in his cupboard during occupational therapy after a mental breakdown. There was nothing in the war record that showed time out for something then considered so shameful, and I was left wondering what the truth might be. I'd known a man who spoke little and seemed unable to have a coherent conversation about anything. In my childhood, he was always sweetly kind and called me his "flower fairy" because I was small and loved flowers, but we were never close. At the war memorial, I found a photo of him with a group of airmen in front of a Lancaster war plane taken during the RAAF liberation of the Philippines. But the best photo of him was a portrait taken at the time he joined up, and I had it printed. I examined the handsome face, the younger man I never knew, the father absent in person and then absent mentally. In my reverie, I left my hat behind.

Parliament House—new since I left Australia in the '60s—is partly constructed into the top of a grand hill with the roof grassed over.

"Such a big-ass flag, babe—your Capitol, eh? It's gorgeous."

The marble foyer impacted both of us with the tall, muted pink and green marble columns and wide staircases. We looked at the walls covered in marquetry panels, and I recognized the waratah flower and eucalyptus leaves and other wild plants. Linda focused on the limestone floor with the masses of ancient marine fossils. The granite and marble, art, and garden, together with ecologically friendly elements, made me feel proud. So impressive yet not grandiose. It wasn't until later that I read of the Aboriginal art and other Australian themes in the decoration of the building.

Linda's fascination with the modern building included an interest in the security and the fact that one simply drove up to the building and parked underneath it.

"Anyone could come in there with fucking explosives."

The few security officers wouldn't let her take photographs. "Go over there so it looks like I's taking your picture, and I can get one a' them security guys."

The artwork at the new Parliament House included an oil painting of a dense forest of white-barked eucalyptus trees. Parallel vertical trunks with variation in height and thickness reminded me of a page of musical notes. It was by Australian painter Arthur Boyd.

"Look, bub, this is an Australian painting I love."

"Yeah, cool. Let's go to the place where they do the government stuff."

In the Great Hall hung a huge tapestry copy of the Boyd painting. It was thirty feet high by sixty-five feet long, filling the front end of the hall. Its huge size took me right into a eucalyptus forest. The weave softened it, as if in a faint mist. One of the guides explained that during the weaving, Halley's Comet was visible, and the weavers added it into the tapestry as a little white splash at the top of the trees. As I gazed, Linda wandered, agog at the grandeur. She held the sixteen-pound silver-and-gilt mace carried by the sergeant-at-arms at the beginning of a day's sitting. We later discovered it was a replica for tourists.

At the gift shop, Linda bought me several mementos, including a big photograph of the tapestry. "I knows you love this, babe. And the place is amazing—you are part of it." I had the picture framed when we got back home, and it remains one of my favorites.

Down the hill in line with the great new building is the original Parliament House—a smaller white "wedding cake" heritage building and home now for Australian art and history. We examined paintings of all the prime ministers from the time of federation in 1901, when the six British self-governing colonies united to form the Commonwealth of Australia. I was interested to see one of my forebears, Sir Edmund Barton, who was involved in writing the Australian Constitution. Linda was full of *I's so proud of you, babe*, and she talked to all the neat, brown-suited women with matching pumps who worked there.

Pointing at me, she said to two of them, "Her great-great-grandfather was the first prime minister of Australia," whereupon the ladies brought over their colleagues to look at me. They smiled broadly but didn't embarrass me further.

Visiting the National Botanic Gardens with Linda and Christina to see all the native plants in flower in the springtime sun was a memorable ending to our trip. We photographed ourselves in front of pink-and-white tea-tree flowers and wandered through the eucalyptus area, rock garden, and banksia garden. Banksias were in full bloom, covered with fat candles of yellow flowers as well as the big gray cylindrical deadheads of last year's flowers, each with scattered open seed cases that looked like lips. As children, we thought these deadheads were rather grim old faces, and Grandpa would say to me, "Watch out, Squizzel, the big bad banksia man will get you." A pair of gray gang-gang parrots with scarlet heads made creaky noises in the rainforest gully; a flock of noisy black white-winged choughs foraged on the eucalyptus lawn. The common sulfur-crested cockatoos screeched, tiny blue fairy wrens in the pink boronias chirruped quietly, and curve-billed honeyeaters and party-colored lorikeets fed at the bottlebrush flowers.

We sat chatting by a garden of Geraldton wax bushes with narrow citrus-smelling leaves and masses of pink and white waxy blooms. Suddenly I saw that strange Australian mammal, the echidna, shuffling under the bushes, poking its long narrow snout into the dirt searching for ants and worms.

"This is a mammal that lays eggs," I said to Linda.

"Yeah, great, eh? I seen it on TV. Looks like a tiny hedge-hog."

Christina and I tended to linger behind Linda, and we didn't need to talk much. I put my arm around her and felt how much I missed her in my faraway Arizona life. Most of the cousins were just names—I had been gone too long. Among my relatives, it was my niece Christina who felt the closest, who shared my intense of love of nature.

We ended up in the Grassy Garden set among granite boulders, where Christina and I reminisced about the trip Reg and I had made to Australia when she and Leonora were teenagers and we picnicked in the bush, cooking our sausages on sticks over the campfire. At last, we moseyed on for tea at the garden café while Linda went to the gift shop to buy me a replacement hat for the one I left at the war memorial.

Our seven weeks came suddenly to an end, and my parting with Christina was tearful. We landed seats in the middle of the plane—one on each aisle with two empty places between us that would allow us to stretch out and sleep. As soon as we were seated, Linda launched into lively mode, talking to anyone who would listen and stopping the flight attendants as they passed by. She looked across at me, and I held up a hand as if to say "later." I knew that back in Arizona, she would say to people, "Liz was telling me shut the fuck up, she tired of me after all this time and won't sit next to me now."

But over the empty seats, she grabbed my hand and said, "Thank you, babe, this whole trip been all so amazing. I loves you so much, and I loves your family."

She settled into a movie while I sat back with eyes shut. It had been good to let the experience recharge my love of Australia. I also felt a deep gratitude for my fortunate child-hood in the much-loved "sunburnt country." It had been heartwarming to see Linda learn and savor so much, to see me with family. In their presence, she had become more her usual talkative, joking self than she had been during the northern part of our trip; it seemed that she found comfort in having familiar people around after all the newness in a strange country.

Back in Tucson on Halloween, John, who was Linda's only family, greeted us at the baggage carousel dressed in a kangaroo suit. He hugged us and seemed pleased to see us both.

THE NEXT DAY, ALONE at my own place, I thought about a conversation I'd had with Linda as we waited for our plane at the Sydney airport. I had asked, "What was the best thing?"

"Your family. Your relatives are great, and you are so lucky. Do you think nature or nurture matters most?"

"Scientists think it's about half and half, and that seems about right to me."

"My birth mother was so bad; it would be great if I found my genetic father and he was someone I could admire."

"Bub. Every family is a mix of different characters. You met my favorite relatives, but there are others—I can think of a con man, a sex abuser, and a narcissist. And for sure the effect of a set of genes can be influenced a lot by parents and teachers."

I watched her as she stared into the distance, silent for once.

10 Back in the Desert

LINDA LAY BESIDE ME on a recliner by the pool. "I's watching that woodpecker guy. He keeps pecking, and he's really loud."

I looked over at her. So brown in her swimsuit, except for white ankles and feet. Such dark brown eyes focused on the tall saguaro cactus. Sun shining through her thick black buzz cut.

The Gila woodpecker was drilling a nest hole in the saguaro. Every day, a fawn head with red hat and big black beak worked the hole bigger and deeper for eggs that wouldn't be laid until the following year. But there was plenty of additional wildlife. Black phainopeplas with their little crests ate red or orange mistletoe fruits and tweeted quietly but persistently in palo verde trees. By midmorning, purple martins, those black crosses in the sky, came swooping down to the pool while we swam, and as dusk approached, bats sailed by.

They were featherbed days, lazing in my desert garden in Tucson after seven weeks in Australia. Novelties of the trip had subdued my talkative sweetheart, while I was often submerged in memories of my Queensland childhood among the eucalyptus forests. But Arizona filled me with nostalgia too.

Before Linda was in my life, Reg and I had spent our last fourteen years together in this rich Sonoran Desert. It hardly seemed a desert at all after the parched and barren regions where we had worked in outback Australia and the Sahara, so we had marveled at every sighting of a bobcat or javelina, every sound of a howling coyote, every flight of the five Harris's hawks that hunted together in our acres. We studied the creosote bush grasshoppers together and wrote up our scientific papers about them. And just for fun, we measured the yearly growth of all our saguaro cactus plants with a tape measure, or triangulation for the tall ones, and plotted out the growth rates of individuals in different size classes. We roamed the desert around our house and examined how the pack rat middens grew quickly in size and the kangaroo rat burrows became gradually longer.

In the golden springtime when palo verde trees blossomed over the hillsides and big buttery cups dotted the prickly pear cactus, we held hands and whispered to each other, "Hasn't it all been wonderful?" Reg died in such a springtime, looking out of our bedroom window with the warm wind full of drifting yellow petals under a clear blue sky.

With Linda, I was again engaged in sharing the details of nature, but this time it was not the knowing soulmate intimacy. It was about opening a ready mind to the fascinations of the desert. It took me back to the time I taught high school in London when I was in my twenties. Classes full of Cockney kids with their rhyming slang tested and teased me with terms I didn't know, but they were full of fun and delightfully hungry for discoveries about the workings of animals. I had been afraid to give them scalpels to dissect anything, but one boy entreated, "Please, miss, me dad's a fishmonger, and I'd bring enough for everyone." I gave in and was thrilled with what transpired. Everybody in the class became so engrossed in looking at gills and guts, air bladders and bones. Each one of them learned more than I'd ever taught from the lectern.

It was a warm evening on the patio when Linda leaned over to me and whispered, "I can hear a puppy." It was an unfamiliar sound, gentler than the hooting of our resident great horned owl or the yapping coyotes. We remained silent, waiting, and when the sound came again, Linda spotted them.

"They's two little birds there—look, sitting on the back of the garden chair!"

A pair of elf owls, barely five inches tall, perched side by side.

It was hard to stay quiet in our excitement as they made their little barking noises before flying off. We saw them on many nights that summer. They were drawn to the light of the house, looking for insects, but they also took scorpions from the rocks of the patio wall.

Best of all that year was the desert cottontail rabbit. We found it as a baby on the road just after a car had run over the mother and apparently squashed out the diminutive thing, still with a wet umbilical cord.

"So tiny and no fur. We gotta save it, babe," Linda urged.

"We'll try, but it mightn't work." We should really have taken it to a rescue place.

"I'll look it up what to do on the pooter."

We went to the store for the nutrients. I had some mini pipettes left over from my lab days and managed to get the baby bunny, eyes shut, to take drops of our synthetic milk. Linda wanted me to do the feeding but loved watching.

"Such a tiny mouth and stuff running out of it."

She didn't want to leave it whenever she went home to the resort but said, "I can't take him, babe. You gotta look after him while I's gone."

I knew it was not that she couldn't but that she was both

unconfident of her ability to do the feeding and unsure of her own reliability. So I kept the miniature bunny in my breast pocket all day, even when I was on campus for classes. I took it out at intervals, clutching the warm body in one hand and dripping the food into its mouth from the pipette with the other. It learned to open a tiny mouth when I touched its lips with the pipette tip.

It turned out to be a female, and Linda named her Pocket. Over the next weeks, her fur grew in soft gray, and as her body filled out, we weighed her on the kitchen scales, where she sat motionless.

"Watch her, babe. Look at her little nose and whiskers twitching."

I kept the records, and Linda would laugh. "You's making a grapht out of it?"

When Pocket opened her protuberant bright eyes, it wasn't long before she turned to look at us when we called her name.

Then her fur grew longer and downy, and as she rested in my hand, fingers lightly closed around her, I felt the thrill of wildness tamed, her neck artery pulsing while she remained motionless. Linda held her for hours. Pocket's main home was a small dog kennel lined with hay and, inside, a cardboard box housing an old T-shirt, where she would hide away, sometimes digging right under the cloth. We would call her, put some fresh leafy food through the door, and watch her hop gingerly out of the box to nibble the treat.

After several weeks, she began to look ragged, with the fur on her chest falling out.

Linda traipsed into my home office, frowning. "Pocket's sick. Gonna leave us."

Then I remembered. "Hey, bub, Pocket needs to eat

mommy poo. Rabbits eat their mother's droppings to get their essential bacteria. We have to collect poo for her."

I found a couple of dozen rabbit droppings in the desert as Linda stood skeptically by, hand on hip. I broke up the very dry pellets into a tiny dish of water from which Pocket could drink, and we kept watch. "She's drinking," Linda called.

About a week later, Linda rushed up, beaming, with Pocket in an outstretched hand. "It worked! She's getting good fur again."

I smiled and stroked the tiny head.

When Pocket was big enough to fill the palm of my hand, we took her out on the patio daily, where she sniffed all the litter and plants, her ears already big but not yet stiff enough to stand up straight. We delighted in every little hop, never letting her out of our sight.

One day, as Linda lazed in the pool, I was busy in the laundry when I saw a gopher snake just outside. I rushed to get Linda. "Come here. Look over in the corner by the laundry door."

The sight of a packrat up on its back legs with a baby suckling struck me as strange, but as I gazed, the snake slowly slid toward her. Then, with a movement almost too fast to see, the snake had the baby, and the mother was gone.

"Oh god, babe, my chest thumping," said horrified Linda, holding on to me, mouth open and eyes wide. "Babe, we gotta be sure one don't get Pocket." I squeezed her hand yes.

Linda had a phobia about snakes and was always on the lookout. "Watch for rattlers," she'd call, or she'd panic about real or imagined serpents around my desert house. "No, it wasn't a pigment of my imagination. Keep your eyes on Pocket." There was a day when she spied a small white eggshell on the ground and didn't see the motionless kingsnake in the nearby hackberry. Five feet of black and white bands were wrapped around branches.

"Sons of bitches, fuck," she shouted as she saw its head beside her and rushed inside to watch it through the window.

WHEN POCKET WAS HALF grown, we had to think about how to let her go. "Can't we keep her?" Linda kissed the top of Pocket's head with tears in her eyes.

"She's a wild animal, bub. She's got to live her life in nature."

Linda cried and whispered, "I love you, Pocket" as she lay on the bed with the bunny resting on her chest. Her eyes, so often full of fun, were soft and gentle now. "I need a long goodbye," she told me, and I bent to kiss them both.

We gave Pocket a soft release. First, we let her out in the enclosed courtyard adjoining the kitchen. The walls were high and gates secure, but there was one small length of low wall topped with metal rods that wouldn't allow coyotes or bobcats through. We followed her from windows as she explored, finding some bursage and other desert plants to nibble as well as a few treats we put out for her. Quail visited, hopping over the little fence, and we went out at intervals to flush out any snake that might have slipped in under a gate. Even Bailey, our Labrador, stood up on her back legs and watched from the window.

I was watching one morning as Linda ambled around in the courtyard. Suddenly, she stood still and beckoned to me. "Come out here!"

She had found a remarkable eighteen quail eggs clumped in the base of a broken-down yucca plant. We kept watch for the next weeks as we followed Pocket. They all hatched, and we often saw the parents with their troop of furry balls.

The parents moved gradually forward as they pecked at the ground, and after a minute or two, the chicks rushed to catch up. Sometimes one of the parents would race back and collect an errant chick. Pocket was oblivious.

Then, one fateful morning, we saw her jump the low wall through the metal poles and into the open desert, where she ran off among the bursage and cactus. Linda and I clutched each other. "Gone!"

Friends said we would never see her again. But amazingly, when we called Pocket the next day, she came back, zigzagging across the desert. We called her for daily treats and took the photos, Linda bending over with a piece of carrot or cilantro in her hand as Pocket stood up on her back paws and reached up for the treat. Other cottontails learned a Pocket call meant food, and after a few weeks, a dozen of them would gather when we called. The highlight of each day was the afternoon feeding. When visitors came, they, too, could call and feed her.

Academic friends from my past life came to visit from around the world. It was a treat for me to talk science and past adventures while Linda enjoyed their animal stories and asked lots of questions. "You study that? What are you going to do with all those butterflies? Is that a British accent? How did you get here from Israel?" She always picked up on something amusing about one of the guests. It would make a story for later.

"That Mike, you know what he said when Liz introduced us? 'Hi, I'm Mike. I have one testicle.' His partner Camille's surname is Parmesan, and he says, 'Take care of Camille Cheddar or Camille Gorgonzola.'"

All of them fell for Pocket—a desert cottontail unafraid to take food from strangers.

Over the year, Pocket grew to full size and had two litters.

We didn't see the kits, but she twice grew plump and then had enlarged, damp teats when she came for food. We searched fruitlessly in her territory for evidence of a nest, but she was too expert at covering up the kits with dirt between suckling times.

Between the two litters, she acquired a long slit in one ear, and I suggested, "Probably from one of the local Harris's hawks." Reg and I had seen the big brown hawks in action—once two birds flushed out a cottontail from under a jojoba bush, and three others chased and caught it. Five hawks shared a meal. It is not uncommon to see the kind of damage that Pocket sustained.

Linda noted, "Well, makes it easy to tell it's Pocket from a distance, eh?"

Whenever we called, the bunny came running, and Linda exclaimed, "Look, here she comes."

It was always a moment of exhilaration when she got close and we could look for anything new—a bit of missing fur, a watery eye, a slight change in fur color. When she developed a couple of lumps on her chest, I knew they were from warble flies. I explained to Linda that these flies lay eggs in the fur, which develop into maggots that dig into the skin.

"Gross."

We saw the lumps only when they were large and the maggots ready to emerge, but the wounds healed, and she was fine.

"All the problems, babe, and they's coyotes and bobcats too."

One hot morning, we called her to us and then spent the day following her and recording all that she did. Because she was unafraid, watching was easy. I followed her slowly as she made her way from under a palo verde tree to the deeper shade under a prickly pear, where she was very hard to see.

There she dug out a hollow in the dry dirt and took a dust bath. As I stood waiting for her next move, I went back to the days in my research career when I had been out in the wilderness watching insect behavior. How curious to now be watching a bunny for fun in just the same way.

I had spent so many days observing caterpillars continuously as I developed theories about their evolution. How interesting it was to discover that plant-feeding insects were so vulnerable to predators and parasites and that feeding led to twenty times more deaths than resting. How important it must be to feed quickly, to have efficient chewing apparatus, to be vigilant. The findings led to understanding that danger of mortality from enemies was much more significant than the much-touted problems with plant food that might be rather toxic or low in nutrients. Watching Pocket was a delight, but so was the memory of all those years of research and discovery.

When it was Linda's turn, she pulled over a little lawn chair and plugged in her earphones for rock music. We monitored everything. Pocket cleaned her fur with her teeth, used her long back legs to wipe over her huge ears, and scratched every part of herself with her feet. She rested often and nibbled a little on a mixture of all the desert shrubs.

At the end of the day, Linda said, "Fuck, babe, we done a long work in a heat wave. I's wackered—can't wait to tell Bobbi how crazy we's been."

For me, there was the data. I still loved to look for what could be extracted from numbers: the biggest proportion of Pocket's day was spent grooming—almost 40 percent. Clearly, keeping her coat in good shape and clear of desert spines and dust was important. A similar time was spent resting, with just a few percent on moving, eating, or digging in the dust.

One day, after about eighteen months, Pocket didn't come when we called. We searched her acre of territory looking for clues. Eventually, Linda yelled, "Come over here." On a big rock, she had found a little heap of intestines. I knew the very long coils could be the remains of a bobcat's meal.

"Bub, bobcats don't care for entrails. A coyote would eat everything. A hawk would have carried her off." It was quite a long life for a desert cottontail but still mournful to accept the demise of a furry little animal that had intoxicated us with her mixture of wildness and passivity.

POCKET'S STORY LIVES ON in three children's books. Linda shot thousands of photos, and she selected the best, while I wrote the text. *Saving Pocket* was the first book, which can be found in Tucson's Pima County Libraries. The second one, *The Pocket Book*, describes how the wild bunny escaped her many potential predators, and the last, *Just Pocket*, tells of all she did through a fourteen-hour summer's day.

While working on the books on a hot day with mourning doves softly cooing in the mesquite, we walked into the Arizona room and looked out onto the patio.

"Babe, there's the bobcat!"

He was resting regally in the forked trunk of the mesquite tree. There is something about size, about big cats and their easy elegance. It had been bobcats that excited Reg more than anything, and we'd kept a record of sightings.

Linda rushed for the binoculars. "He's been in a fight. Got a front paw tore open." He rested in the tree for a couple of hours, and we had time to take in the big brown body, unusually orange face ruff, spots on his chest and legs. He panted, licked his wounds, and gazed into the distance. When he limped to the pond at the side of the house, we watched him through the glass door of the bedroom, slowly lapping. "I wonder how he got hurt, bub."

"He must be the one that got Pocket. Oh, babe, but he is gorgeous."

Whenever we saw a desert cottontail, Linda would say slowly and sadly, "Pocket." For years, friends, former classmates, and colleagues inquired, "How is Pocket?" Or smiled, saying, "I remember you with that little Pocket bunny."

As I CONTINUED WITH classes for the MFA, I had Linda read some of my writings as well as essays by younger students. She enjoyed being included and learning about people from their writings. At parties held for classes, Linda made friends with the gay students.

After one party, she grabbed me. "I's so envious of those lesbian couples—so young and already in relationships."

Long after the classes had ended and the students dispersed across the country, she kept in touch with Molly and Katie and their partners. She loved animals, but people interested her most. Her attachment to these women was an expression of her yearning for the fuller long-term lesbian relationship so frustratingly out of reach for most of her life.

She grabbed me after one of the parties. "Babe, I loves you, but we been shafted."

"Shafted?"

"Yeah, we don't have so much time. And we lost Pocket. We gotta hold on to everything."

For Linda, the special love of all things wild had been awakened in her just by looking. Nature had always topped the list of things that mattered to me, not just for interest and curiosity but because it produced numinous experiences that gave my life meaning. E. O. Wilson, in *Biophilia*, suggests that all of us have an innate tendency to seek connection with nature. For me, the love of butterflies when I was very young marked the beginning of my journey. Linda found a connection to wildlife later in life. I wondered if it would continue or acquire intensity. With attention deficit syndrome, she had a penchant for anything new and different—surely nature would continue to provide sufficient novelty. But would I?

11 The Entomologist

IT WASN'T THE FIRST time that Linda complained, "Why didn't you study something interesting like koalas or dolphins?" How could I explain why insects were so fascinating and why I became an entomologist? If she saw a bug, she would stomp on it and then point to the dead insect. "What's that?"

One mosquito bite drove her crazy. Anything that could bite was attracted to her, and she was quickly exasperated. "What the fuck got me this time? You gotta look at it with a telescope"—her joke name for my Opti visor.

As far back as I could remember, insects had interested me, even the blood-feeders, whose bites rarely bothered me. Linda didn't believe me when I first told her we didn't have window screens in my Queensland childhood home, and mosquitoes always swarmed under the dining table and under the bed. She did laugh, though, when I told her that my brother Barton and I competed to see who could kill the most mosquitoes during dinner. We made little piles of corpses beside our plates while our father laughed, undercutting Mother's sense of propriety.

But Linda did like butterflies. We watched the common black-and-blue *Battus* swallowtails laying eggs on the red-brown leaves of their hostplant. Then as the eggs hatched into bright-red caterpillars, they finished chewing up the plant and wandered off, looking for more of the same.

"They really going to find food, babe? They's no more plants here."

"They're really good at finding their special plant." We found a specimen of the rather cryptic plants just a few yards away and watched as one of the scarlet creatures zigzagged toward it and began feeding immediately.

"Well, why're they red? You'd think birds'd see them easily."

"It is interesting—these guys feed only on that special plant, and it's got poisons the caterpillars like. After eating the plant, they keep all the poisons in their bodies, and that protects them from predators."

"Cool."

From then on, Linda had an eye out for both the caterpillars and the butterflies. "*Battus,*" she would call, "*Battus,* over there." She learned all the common butterfly species—painted ladies, queens, Gulf fritillaries, citrus swallowtails. I loved to watch her looking out for any new species, those shapely brown boy-legs wandering among the desert plants, her quick eyes spotting butterflies from a distance as I thought back to my childhood when I chased green and yellow birdwings though my mother's flower garden.

We both liked painted ladies best, the most widely distributed butterfly species in the world. Black and orangey brown with white spots, they were easy to identify, and sometimes there were swarms of them. In spring, we found a few of their caterpillars on a thistle plant. Dark and covered with soft little projections, they had constructed a house by weaving together a few leaves so that the treacherous spines would repel their ant predators.

"How do they know to do that?"

"They're programmed. The ones that are good at it live to make babies; the others are likely to get eaten, so the good builders produce more good builders."

"Wow, babe!" Her little brown face looked at me wide-eyed as the sun shining on her black hair reminded me of woolly bear caterpillars with their fuzz of black.

I smiled and told her about my student Dana. "He found that painted ladies migrate north from Mexico in spring and lay eggs on thistles in Arizona, where ants are their biggest problem, and the ants have trouble getting to the caterpillars in their armed houses. When these caterpillars become butterflies, they continue north and use lupines for food and get protection because of the poisons in lupine leaves. Birds are their main enemies in Washington, and they don't like the taste of lupine-filled caterpillars."

"Well! They do different things in different places?"

"Amazing, eh? Adaptation to different kinds of predators."

I was thrilled with Dana's work at the time because I felt that predators could drive the evolution of insect herbivores, and here was a great example of local predators influencing butterfly behavior in different ways. In fact, life for the plant-feeders, including what foods they prefer and how many species they feed on, has been determined to a large extent by their natural enemies.

AFTER A BUTTERFLY CHILDHOOD, I had taken a break from anything entomological as I went through a couple of bohemian years, travels in Europe, and high-school teaching in London, but I eventually returned to insects, obtaining higher degrees at the University of London. There, I met

Reginald Chapman, my life's love. As one of England's big names in entomology, he was writing *The Insects: Structure and Function*, which would ultimately make him famous in his field. I became his principal reader, and we spent many happy hours discussing how to make all the physiology accessible yet accurate. He was rather odd-looking with his flat face, mole on cheek, and slightly prognathous jaw, but his quiet enthusiasm totally charmed me, and I came to love his appearance. During our first months as lovers, I spent evenings making an index for his eight-hundred-page book while he was teaching. I wrote down words and page numbers from the first printed copy on a hundred sheets of foolscap paper spread out over the floor. Our nearly forty years together were lives of shared research, love of music and literature, wordless empathy. After he died, it was Linda who raised me out of despair and misery. I was enchanted with her light-hearted humor and increasing engagement with natural history, including an interest in the six-legged creatures that had made my career.

AT THE BEGINNING OF summer in Tucson, many moths and beetles emerge from their winter hiding places, and most of them fly at night. We saw an elf owl catch moths on the patio. We found moths at the lights above doors and even on the uncovered windows, and in the mornings, we found the last moths resting on outside walls. I arranged for us to go with my avid insect-collector friend, Margarethe, on a blacklight trip.

Margarethe erected a large white sheet that hung vertically in a clearing in the mountains south of Tucson. The blacklight is a special bulb that sends out UV light as well as visible wavelengths, which attracts a lot more insects than an ordinary incandescent bulb. She had a generator and pointed the light toward the sheet.

Linda peered at the bright sheet. "Black light's a weird name for all this shining!"

It didn't take long for the first arrivals.

"Oh, look at that beautiful geometrid moth," called Margarethe, pointing to a delicate green moth with white lines across its wings.

"Oh yeah, *Nemoria obliqua*, I think," called one of the other entomologists.

I was surprised when a border patrol van came by without even stopping. Margarethe smiled. "They never stop. They're used to entomologists with blacklights because this is such a famous collecting area."

Next came the hawk moths, mostly the white-lined sphinx, and a host of smaller moths, some of them very pale and delicate. Linda was speechless as hordes of moths accumulated on the sheet, and a couple of other collectors with us took their pick, pushing their favorites into vials. But Margarethe was most interested in beetles, and they came a bit later.

"That's a looker," Linda shouted as the first big green scarab beetle arrived. The shiny beetles plopped onto the sheet by the dozen and crawled all over it, disturbing the smaller moths. Linda couldn't take her eyes off the entomological mass, with all their colors and different sizes and shapes. By eleven, the sheet was covered with a vast array of moths, bugs, beetles, and other insects. It was heaven for the insect collectors, and Linda gazed at the sheet: "Wow, just wow!"

But it wasn't the end. The very late arrivals tended to be larger, and there were giant silk moths that seemed to just float into the light and gently land on top of the mass. They were *Polyphemus* moths, bigger than my hand. Their beige background was interrupted by a black band and a multi-colored central eyespot on each wing. One was a male, as demonstrated by the very feathery antennae containing the organs for smell to detect female sex pheromones. No one spoke. It was a moment of absorption in nature's glory—so many, so varied, so beautiful, and almost no part of the sheet uncovered. Linda turned to me with a grin. "They's fucking amazing."

Back home, Linda began looking with new eyes. She found the scarlet bugs that suck young mesquite shoots and shot striking photos of them. Then the milkweeds with red and black sucking bugs at the seeds, queen butterflies at the flowers, and the orange masses of aphids clustered around the buds. She was naturally observant, and it was satisfying, too, that she had taken to the idea of insects.

There were other attractions though. When we found a dead Cooper's hawk, Linda commanded, "Pick that up. I gotta have the feathers."

I laughed. "You pick it up if you want them so badly."

Together we put the body on the flat roof of my house. Then we dragged a wheelbarrow up the steps to the roof and inverted it over the hawk to prevent scavengers from stealing it. After it dried out, we put it in a paper bag in the laundry room and forgot about it. Months later, my kitty, Bowtie, tore open the bag and released a lot of drab little moths from among the dust of half-eaten feathers.

"Oh, babe, you the biologist, you let this happen!"

"Sorry, bub, but it is really interesting. These tineid moths are important for breaking down this kind of stuff. There are little beetles eating the feathers too. Think natural recycling."

She looked sadly at the mass of spoiled feathers. "At least we can get the skull."

Linda was not a morning person, but on one occasion,

I got her to walk out in the desert early, after a night of rain. Thousands of leafcutter ants were swarming—dark chocolate-colored insects swirling in dense columns ten and twenty feet high. As we walked along the winding road, we saw more of them, perhaps a swarm every thirty yards, the distant ones like plumes of smoke rising from the creosote bushes.

"Look, bub, they're paired up in the swarm."

"Yeah."

And as we watched, males captured females, and they fell together to the ground, creating a seething mass of black sex life on the moist desert earth below, shedding their wings as they crawled about. Linda bent to look closer at the frantic activity.

I pointed at one already half-buried. "See the females, digging to make new nests?"

"What happens to the boys?"

"They just die. The girls will be queens. They carry a special fungus, and in the new nest, they will plant the fungal spores so that it grows and provides the new colony with food."

"They lay eggs down there?"

"Yes, hundreds. And those eggs hatch into worker ants that tend the queen and fungus garden."

"Very cool."

As we turned for home, the swarms were all grounded. Linda stopped. "Look at them quail and cactus wrens pecking up their breakfast."

The next spring, when palo verde trees were flowering, we watched another part of the leafcutter ant story. Yellow trails of fallen flowers led away from the trees.

"See how worker ants are carrying them along a chemical path they made to the underground nests? They drop some on the way, and that creates a trail of yellow. Worker ants nourish the fungus gardens with chewed-up petals."

I wondered aloud, "How many people know that beneath their feet, perhaps six yards down, a colony of millions, in thousands of chambers, have an egg-laying queen and monster fungus gardens? That they live in a space the size of a house, and dozens of such colonies occur in just an acre!"

Linda was impressed. "I love you, babe; you just love this shit, eh?" But there was a limit to how much detail she wanted to absorb. "Look, there's a pepla guy up in that tree."

Linda's fascination with the newness of the desert quickly evolved. It became so much more than just a place where things stick into skin, or sting, or bite. It made me love her more— Linda, the fascinating, intermittent sweetheart in my house becoming a naturalist, an entomologist even.

There were times when insects took second place. At a dude ranch near the settlement of Yucca in central Arizona, masses of yucca plants were in flower, and I looked in some of the white bell-shaped blooms, searching for the famous yucca moths. Their story can be found in every book on pollination or co-evolution. I had once spent days chasing yuccas for visiting Chinese colleagues who were desperate to see the moths.

"Look, bub, these little white guys make neat bundles of pollen with their front legs and actually pollinate flowers by putting the little ball of pollen on a new flower by hand." But Linda was focused on horses. We galloped across the yucca-covered desert and along the dry washes, scaring the occasional jackrabbits, which leapt away like small deer.

"Love the horsies, babe," shouted Linda above the wind and thumping of horses' hooves.

"Love the yuccas too," I called back.

AT MY HOME IN the desert, my private nature preserve, our lives were bound together with love for all that we could watch and imagine, learn about, and listen to. It could be a new bird call, a new javelina sighting, a bobcat bringing its young, a desert spiny lizard pumping up and down, a Gulf fritillary butterfly laying eggs on passion vine. With insects now a part of the repertory, we were often bent over examining small ones: harvester ants carrying seeds to their nests, assassin bugs sucking the juice out of a hapless caterpillar.

We did get mosquitoes occasionally. As soon as Linda saw one on her bare leg and successfully slapped it dead, she'd say, "Look, blood. That's *my* blood. Well, let's look at the damn sucker."

I took out my old microscope and showed her how to adjust the focus and distance between the eyepieces.

"Long stripy legs, babe."

"Look at the front end, the tiny head."

"Yeah, he's got antennae."

"It's a girl. Only the girls have that proboscis to dig into you. It's made up of six tiny flexible needles. Two of them do the sawing into you, two hold the incision open, and two of them make a kind of straw to suck the blood."

"No wonder they kill me."

As I CONTINUED WITH classes and workshops in writing after retirement as an entomologist, Linda met my teachers in the English department and came to the parties. But with her newfound enthusiasm for insects and other wild animals, Linda was most thrilled to meet my biology colleagues. Alex was a favorite. This handsome Russian not only studied evolution and all the animals in the desert but was a famous wildlife photographer and kindly spent time with her as she photographed a great horned owl family in a Tucson palm tree. She worked for months until the chicks finally left the nest. We kept up with Alex and often checked the spectacular photography on his website.

We visited Dan working in the Santa Rita Mountains on butterflies. One of his students, squatting by an Ambrosia plant, proceeded to tell us about the chemicals in the plant and exactly how the caterpillars metabolized them. As we moved on, Linda said, "Did you get all that? I heard *blah blah blah*."

Nancy talked about the aphids living in globular galls at the base of cottonwood leaves and how the youngest offspring became little soldiers defending the rest of the colony from their lookout at a small hole in the gall. Steve talked about his bees, Noah his Drosophila flies. Visitors from around the world who came to stay with me in Tucson were a constant source of interest.

Thomas from Germany came to work with me and one of my students on tiger moth caterpillars and how they taste and sequester the special chemicals they need. Linda had earlier helped me collect the caterpillars, but she was most fascinated by Thomas's German university title of "professor doctor." Linda began calling me "Professor Doctor," and when she discovered I had two doctorates, it became "Professor Doctor Doctor." It always made her laugh.

Among my emails one morning came a notice that the celebrated Professor Bert Hölldobler was to visit the University of Arizona and show his prize-winning documentary about ants—*Ants: Nature's Secret Power*. Linda was as enthusiastic as I was, and we arrived on campus with time to spare.

"I am on campus! And look at you—strutting around the minute you put one foot on university ground." Linda laughed with exaggerated swaggering as she looked back at me. She was in excited mode, and I smiled at her imagination; no one strutted less than I did. We found the big room in the students' union, where a crowd had already assembled, but we got seats near the front. Bert was up on the stage and saw me. He waved and called out, "Hi, Liz."

Linda was overjoyed. "I'm with her," she said jokingly to the people around us.

I smiled and took her hand as we settled in for the movie.

While Bert was introducing the film, a cell phone rang, and he was furious: "Who is that?"

A small gray-haired lady, who turned out to be his wife, stood up and said softly, "It's your phone, dear" as she quickly turned it off. The tittering was brief, and the moment passed, but not before Linda had concocted a story about the phone to tell later. "Funniest goddamn thing."

At the end of the documentary, Linda turned to me with sparkling eyes. "We gotta get a copy of that, babe. It's so amazing; I want to watch it over again."

WHEN LINDA WAS BACK at the resort with John, I often sat among the saguaros and let the sound of mourning doves become part of the sadness that losing Reg left me with—the intellectual and emotional splendor with a loved partner who died too soon. How in the laboratory, we'd learned the way locusts control their food intake via one tiny nerve to the esophagus. How in India, we'd watched pest caterpillars on sorghum crops and discovered that leaf surface wax in resistant varieties contained chemicals that altered their behavior, making the newly hatched babies toss their lives away into the breeze instead of climbing down into the heart of the plant to eat. How we'd discovered the way a colorful grasshopper in Nigeria avoided being poisoned by the cyanide in the cassava leaves that they relished. We had puzzled over insect physiology questions as we drank our late-night pints of warm beer at the Carpenter's Arms in London or drank our morning tea as we sat on a Tucson patio, watching Harris's hawks.

In my new life, though, I had a new, warm feeling. My inquiring sweetheart had taken on desert life, including insects. She had also taken on me as biologist and as writer, who she would often find sitting at a computer. My entomological life in Tucson and around the world with Reg became subjects for the creative nonfiction I wrote for my new degree. Linda read several of the essays and pointed out some problems. "What do ya mean here?"

As some of my thesis chapters were published, Linda would hug me. "You's my special professor doctor (but not a real one), and I loves you." At the resort, she would say, "Hi, this my friend. She's a bug professor." The stories I had written about life with insects and Reg eventually became a book published years later: *Six Legs Walking: Notes from an Entomological Life*, enabling Linda to say, "You's a entomologist *and* a writer!"

We sat on my patio on a warm summer evening, enjoying the sound of distant coyotes and the faint fluttering of long-nosed bats at the hummingbird feeder. I thought back to the joint love of insect biology with Reg and how automatically we shared a fascination with the lives and workings of that most diverse group of animals. It was different but rewarding with Linda, whose interest had grown over time, and I'd enjoyed the thrill of being an advocate.

I wondered if Linda's new enthusiasm for desert natural history was a way for her to relate to me through the things I loved. Or was it more an expression of her own potent natural curiosity and interest in discovery? Irving Biederman and Edward Vessel provide evidence for opioid receptor involvement in how our brains crave information; Linda might provide an exemplar. Perhaps the times outside in my semi-wilderness unconsciously provided some of the well-known benefits of nature for health and happiness. I would never know the answers for sure with respect to Linda, but I am high on the Nature Relatedness Scale and was elated at how natural history was becoming a knot that helped to tie the strings of our disparate lives.

12 Giving

LINDA RUSHED INTO MY house carrying a bunch of red roses.

"For you, babe; it's our anniversary." Her face was flushed as she beamed at me.

I hugged her with the roses in one hand and kissed her on the cheek. No one else had ever given me a bunch of red roses. I could remember just one occasion when I was given a lot of flowers, long before I met Linda. I had been to Australia to see family, leaving Reg in Tucson with twenty frozen dinners, and when I returned, he had filled the whole house with blue irises, my favorites. A hundred welcoming blooms brought tears of adoration to my exhausted eyes.

But red roses! Every month, Linda wanted to celebrate the thirteenth day—the monthly celebration of our first night together. I was charmed by her uninhibited romanticism and felt slightly guilty for being more pragmatic. I had never been very good at showing affection, and celebratory gifts had never been important in my life, even in childhood. There had been a few special occasions, like the time Mother and I passed a secondhand store when I was five, and we looked in the window and saw a little old tricycle. I didn't ask for it, but as we walked on, she saw the tears running down my cheeks, and she turned us back to buy it. In general, gifts had been few and frugal.

I never had birthday parties and went to very few. Mother told me, "Darling, they are virtually requests for presents, and I think that's vulgar." She knew that the kids from wealthy families would bring the expensive gifts to birthday parties that highlighted inequities. She also understood that big giving was often self-serving, a view written about by many psychologists. Recent articles by British science writer David Robson provide ample evidence that conspicuous giving and too-obvious altruism arouse suspicion that the giver is doing it to obtain the admiration of others. My mother's views left their mark, ensuring I devalued gifts and instilling in me a preference for anonymity when I contribute to causes.

Mother didn't believe in celebrating the commercial Mother's Day either, instead observing the church's traditional Mothering Sunday, when we had simnel cake. "No presents, children—just pick a few daisies from the garden." I would rush out, pick a few flowers, and make her a posy. Although she was not concerned with material goods, she was warmly emotional, and we were very close. Together, we admired the drifting butterflies from the terrace and read books on the veranda. She loved hearing everything about my days at school and couldn't hear enough about what the teachers taught me.

It was also Mother who first inspired my curiosity about the world. We were kneeling by the side of the long flowerbed, where we dug into the rich earth with our garden trowels to make rows of holes that I moistened with a dribble of water from the hose. She unwrapped the parcels—first a roll of newspaper and then a piece of old Hessian, exposing seedling plants with their roots embedded in damp sawdust. We would each free one and suspend it in one of our holes and then push earth around the roots until it stood firm.

"Mama, how do these flowers grow?"

"Just from water and dirt and air."

The idea completely captured my eight-year-old imagination, and the mystery of how plants and animals effected their magic became a lifelong passion.

She found me wanting in a particular way. "Darling, you are so undemonstrative," she complained as she stroked my bare legs while I stood beside her, waiting patiently to run away. I found such physical fondness awkward. My father rarely showed emotion at all, and having met a variety of his relatives, I suspect I inherited something of his reserve. So many were aloof, and there were all the spinsters who seemed distant. Were they shy, uninterested, or too diffident to express warmth?

THE PRESENT-GIVING IN OUR family at Christmas was limited to very small items—an embroidered handkerchief, a pair of socks, a fountain pen. We put them on one another's placemats to be opened after returning from church for our breakfast. We had no Christmas tree, but we hung branches of eucalyptus over the doorways and brought out all the specially polished silver dishes and cutlery for the table. The big thing was the lunch. It was summer and always hot, so we had cold roast chicken, which was a luxury in my childhood of cheap lamb and mutton. There was also ham, potato salad, and a big bowl of tomato and lettuce. My sister, Jennifer, and I spent the morning making a huge tropical fruit salad for dessert, cutting up papaya, pineapple, banana, mango, passionfruit, oranges. Presents were nothing compared with the feast eaten around the big cedar table shrouded in white damask linen and adorned with all that family silver.

"Who's going to pull my cracker with me?" my little brother, Adrian, would call. I'd lean over the table to pull a paper cracker that looked like a ten-inch bonbon. It made a snapping and tearing sound, and out fell a paper crown, a joke on a slip of paper, and a blow-out noisemaker. Father and my sister, Jennifer, always pulled each other's crackers, leaving our mother to pull hers with my older brother, Barton.

"Christ, these jokes are moronic," he declared.

Mother looked severely at him. "Barton! Mind your words."

"Well, only a dimwit would think they're funny."

As we ate, we wore our paper crowns self-consciously but pretended it was all fun. I suspect the attempt at gaiety in a family that tended to be sullen rather than jolly was related to financial stresses that suffocated my parents' relationship and influenced us all. The money problem was finally revealed when I was in high school: bailiffs called to announce an impending eviction. No one had suspected that my very secretive father had accumulated a vast debt, though Mother struggled to keep the household running with the weekly housekeeping he gave her. Much later, I discovered that eight years of exorbitant fees for my private girls' school were a large part of the problem. She had so badly wanted that excellent school for me. He was unable to tell her it was unaffordable.

BIRTHDAY PRESENTS WERE INTERMITTENT, and because my birthday is on New Year's Eve, the card on my Christmas present often read, "Merry Christmas and Happy Birthday." I do remember feelings of disappointment early on, but I ended up thinking that it didn't really matter. The year I turned

ten, my parents forgot my birthday altogether, and I told myself that gifts and birthday wishes didn't count. I knew my
family cared deeply about me. Perhaps though, somewhere
in my brain, these childhood experiences etched a certain dis-
regard for presents.

Then there had been Reg. We shared the deepest togetherness, but we never bought gifts for each other. Instead, we
bought music, books, or art together. We chose tickets for the
symphony and opera together. Our birthdays were celebrated
in elegant restaurants, lingering for the evening, raising our
wine glasses, and feeling the depth of our affection in each
other's eyes. Later, as he lay dying in the Tucson springtime,
I sat beside him while yellow petals drifted outside our bedroom window. He grasped my hand. "Lizzie, it was all inside
our heads, wasn't it?"

LINDA LOVED TO BUY me presents, though. It was part of
her language of love and a new experience for me. I was
touched by her giving and loved her for it but sometimes
worried. "Bub, you can't keep buying me things."

She would reply, "I loves you, babe, and I want you to
have these things from me."

I would hold her tenderly, wondering how to reciprocate.

The gifts I wanted to provide were more about the joy of
experiences without the accumulation of chattels, though the
mementos she gave me kept accumulating. I have photos in
small frames, a silver heart, an inscribed stone, posters, post-
cards, mugs, and T-shirts. She particularly loved to give me
books like *A Birder's Guide to Southeastern Arizona*.

I took her to the Oasis bookstore in Tucson, where we
browsed for a while before she bought me Richard Shelton's *Going Back to Bisbee*. We were at Oasis to hear one of

my other writing professors read from his new book. Fenton Johnson talked about life in the Kentucky hills, personal retreats, and the surprising value of celibacy. Linda, with her short attention span, spent much of her time counting tiles on the ceiling. But she had taken in more of the reading than I had imagined. "I gotta get you a copy so you get an A."

She lined up for *Keeping Faith: A Skeptic's Journey* and an autograph, and when she got to the desk, she said to Fenton, "Yeah, I agree with you about celibacy."

He was excited and began to expound further, whereupon Linda grinned. "Oh, I just meant celibacy till we got out to the car."

She had no idea that paying attention to my teacher was not going to affect my grades, but she was thrilled to have bought the book for me. It was then that I realized how the giving was not just to please me—giving made her smile and laugh with pleasure. She really loved to give.

Linda also just liked buying things or getting me to buy them. As she inspected my simple kitchen, she wanted me to shop for an electric kettle, a chopper, a coffeemaker—all of them seemed unimportant, but I laughed and got them anyway and often used them. Gone were the days of yearning to be a minimalist.

We celebrated the three-year anniversary of our first night together at a dude ranch. "Happy anniversary, babe," she said, giving me a little white box. I opened it slowly and took out an iPod Shuffle.

"I want you to have it cos I love mine. And I've put your music on it."

I kissed her on the cheek. "Bublet, your sweet gifts! And I'm really getting into the gadgets now, eh?"

She grinned as she showed me how to turn it on. I hopped

around wearing the earphones and waving my arms, making her explode with laughter at my clumsy dancing. "Babe, you so silly." I cruised off on a solitary morning walk listening to Bach, leaving her in bed with Simon and Garfunkel.

She loved all her electronic stuff and always had an eye on new models of Apple computers, iPads, or iPhones. She gave me her old phone when she got a new one. In Tucson, we wandered through the street fairs. "Buy them floppy pants," Linda demanded after the first time I had bought a pair at the Fourth Street fair, and we again saw a tent with rows of the things. Although she didn't try to influence my clothing choices, she had taken a fancy to the pants, and I ended up with four pairs of them: wide-legged, brightly patterned rayon pants with elastic at the ankle. Linda liked boy's clothes herself, and I usually wore plain long pants and blouses. But I took to the baggy things and wore them often for a few years.

We stopped at all the photography stalls, where she was mostly unimpressed. "Look at that. What terrible balance! What bad focus!"

At the tent of our friend Margarethe, we admired her watercolors of nature and pets and flicked through all the greeting cards decorated with paintings of butterflies and beetles.

"Gotta buy you some packets a' them."

She liked to buy me things at such fairs when I wasn't looking. On one occasion, I was busy tasting different chili peppers and buying the obligatory tri tip beef from BBQ 4 U when she bought me a T-shirt with insect designs on the front. Another time she got me a set of four handmade prints of plants with insect visitors: my favorite was one of thistles with butterflies, but all four of them went up on my wall.

Traveling was a great time for Linda to buy me stuff. She

got me a leather shoulder bag in Montreal, a steel tuatara in New Zealand, a shirt in Fiji. In Hawaii, she bought me a square bowl made of teak inlaid with swirls of coconut and palm wood. It sat on my long mesquite bookcase, where Bowtie liked to survey the living room and pounce on toy mice. With it on the bookcase were two bronzes: a foot-high jackrabbit by Mark Rossi that Reg and I bought in Tucson and an enlarged, cup-sized bronze sculpture of a butterfly egg made by a sculptor in Mendocino, California.

As Linda became more involved with nature photography, she printed and framed photos for me of colorful insects, hummingbirds flying, scenes from our motor home trips. She made me a miniature photo album with shots of my old cat, Tigger, and then another of little Bowtie kitty pouncing, climbing, and leaping.

I ENJOYED BEING THE recipient of Linda's gifts. But it wasn't just objects. "I gotta take you to Vegas, babe. It's so much fun."

She looked at me with wide eyes and talked fast about all the crazy excesses, the luxury, the casinos, the restaurants (though she wouldn't eat in most of them—"too foo foo"). I had never been tempted by Las Vegas with its reputation for garishness, waste, and brashness, but eventually I agreed to go. As a discount specialist, she booked us into the Venetian casino and resort with a cut-rate deal. The biggest hotel in the United States was as luxurious as anything I had ever experienced. I looked around our room at soft beige curtains, paintings of the ocean on one wall and four abstract pieces on another, a gray sofa across from purple armchairs, a large coffee table with picture books, an oak desk and ergonomic chair.

"Look, babe, here's a panel. You can control any light or close the curtains."

I went into the marble bathroom and washed my hands with Estee Lauder White Linen soap, squeezed out a little La Mer Hand Treatment, and pocketed a Puff's paper tissue.

In the gaming space at the Venetian, almost three acres of plush carpet lit from enormous chandeliers were filled with table games and slot machines. Long legs and immense cleavages of cocktail waitresses glided along the lanes, offering free drinks. We learned to play craps in this astonishing atmosphere, and we were soon drawn into the fun of it. A group of twelve players leaned on the ledges of the oval table, where the box man and several supervisors kept a beady eye on the complex procedures. Linda learned the many details quickly and gave me instructions. "Careful to throw the dice gently so it don't bounce off the table. Don't bet on dice number combinations." The game was lively because all the players got excited when anyone beat the house, leading to a camaraderie peculiar to the game. There were many ways to bet, but I stuck with the easiest choices, settling on the pass line that offered the best odds. Linda won seventy dollars, and I won thirty.

We watched the gondolas in blue chlorine-clean canals, and Linda's eyes danced with delight as she rushed me along. "I's taking you to St. Mark's Square—they's got real opera singers there, so you can even get your opera songs!" I found it astonishing. Unlike actual Venice, it all looked brand new. On the strip, we watched people decked out in every kind of garb—gay men in skirts and scarlet high heels, young people dressed as pop stars, teenagers on stilts, elderly couples in exotic evening dress with boas and sequins, all enjoying being outrageous in this crazy place. It was fun, despite the noise and visual extravaganza, though Linda sensed my underlying distaste.

"Well, it is amazing, and people with no money can come and see all this for *nothing*."

That got my attention. Showy pageants have an appeal for most of us at some level, and Reg and I had loved the elaborate, historic ceremonies in England, and we made sure his children, Anne and Philip, had a chance to enjoy them also. For Linda, it was not just the displays, amusements, and over-the-top element in Las Vegas. The variety alone kept her sparkling: people, clothes, behavior, shows, lights, games. "Babe, look at her. Jeez, that magician with a monkey! Wait, gotta get a shot of that crazy lady with pink fur to the ground!" I wondered if her love of variety might have some relationship to her inability to stay focused—her self-confessed attention deficit syndrome—but perhaps it was simply her uncommon ability to handle multiple sensory inputs that underlay a gleeful engagement with a mountain of them in Las Vegas.

She bought me a red fleece pullover with "Las Vegas" embroidered on the left where there might have been a pocket. "You gotta have something from Vegas, babe." Later, she gave me a little silver-framed photo of us wearing jeans in St. Mark's Square as we stood beside a pair of opera singers in extravagant *La Traviata* garb.

BACK IN TUCSON, WITH Linda away at the resort, I spent a day on my patio under the big mesquite tree with Bowtie on a leash beside me. My head was still full of Las Vegas, and the birds were just background. Every scene came back: Linda rushing to the next sight, looking at me with big eyes and a wide smile. "Just look, babe, look at that." She had been triumphant that I had had fun despite myself, that she had engaged my interest in a place she loved. I smiled to myself as I thought about her desire to include me and share her excitement. And I did have fun. I felt open to change in the new life that was so different from all that had come before, and it had taken passionate Linda, my remarkable sweetheart, to open the windows I had never cared to look through.

PRESENTS HAD BEEN A huge part of Linda's life. Adoring parents and then husband John had given her so many—toys, bikes, dogs, horses, motorcycles, cars. I probably only heard about a fraction of them, but it was clear they were expressions of affection from the three people who had mattered through most of her life. It made sense that she wanted to do the same for me, but the contrast with my own life couldn't have been greater.

Linda made me think about giving. Many animals bestow gifts on each other. Typically, they are nuptial gifts that enhance the likelihood of successful mating. But there are a few recorded cases with crows apparently having fun with gifts and bonobos giving food to strangers in the expectation of yet more interaction in these ultra-social little apes. Gift-giving occurs among chimpanzees, and it is believed that this helps to form bonds and build trust. Perhaps this was the original function in early humans also, though anthropologists consider that the gifting in the earliest humans was probably more about status or dominance in the giver.

In my relationship with Linda, I was grateful for all the ways she showed affection, including her penchant for giving me presents. I loved her for it because it was her nature to express affection that way and because the giving gave her such pleasure. And I developed much enjoyment in finding gifts for her, like Leica binoculars for birding. The biggest joy for me was providing new experiences, learning new things together, expanding horizons, sharing ideas, reading the same books so we could talk about them. For Linda, material items and dramas remained enticing, but she developed a bigger interest in what lay beyond them.

13 Finding Balance

IT WAS A FEBRUARY morning. A male Anna's hummingbird flew out of an acacia, hovered briefly, and then climbed to well over one hundred feet. He dived straight down, the sun reflecting off his iridescent red throat and head. He abruptly pulled up, making an explosive squeaky pop before circling back to his bush.

Linda looked at me. "Wow, babe, so proud of hisself. Why's he doing that?"

"He does it for the girl, but I don't see her. Confident though, eh?" I replied, thinking how Linda's drollery hid her lack of confidence despite having been an accomplished photojournalist. But she liked being with someone who had gone further and into a world unknown to her.

"I never met a professor before I met you, and I feel proud to be with you, builded up by being your partner. Before, I knew people liked John, and that made me feel I was liked because I was with him. I feel builded up when I am with someone important."

I was humbled. "Bub, you are special to me," I assured her.

On top of my good fortune in having had teachers who turned my academic life around, I had Reg, who credited me with more than I thought I was worth, encouraged my inventive mind, and helped to make me the scientist I became. He gave up a successful career in England for me to take up a professorship in Berkeley. Linda, though, never had that kind of soulmate. She had John. I could perhaps be for Linda what Reg had been for me, at least with respect to inspiring interest in learning details of the natural world, and this thought animated our interactions when she was not too distracted by something else.

We rested on a rock to watch Harris's hawks with fluffed brown feathers on the top of a saguaro. "Be great if they got something right in front of us," Linda hoped. Then a Cooper's hawk flashed by with a dove in its claws.

"Look, bub, there's Coopie; he's a bird hawk. Look how good he is at flying through tight spaces in the mesquite tree." It had become a hawk day. But Linda was distracted. "Listen. I hear sirens. One is a fire engine, and there's two police cars." I hadn't noticed, any more than I noticed planes flying overhead, but sirens and alarms never failed to arouse her attention. In her mind, she returned to Texas, where she had seen so many people hurt or killed, reliving the adrenaline rush and a need to record everything with her camera.

LINDA KNEW ABOUT ALL things mechanical, and that helped to make her feel valued. "You don't need to pay for people to fix stuff, babe. I's the guy."

We were on the road in her motor home between Pagosa Springs in Colorado and Chama in New Mexico when we heard a deafening bang. Linda pulled off the road, and I jumped out to look. "There's been an explosion. Maybe the propane tank."

Linda knew better. "A blowout, one a' the inside tires."

She checked for other damage. The worst was the exhaust pipe, bent double and no longer functional. "Getting late, babe. Gotta get this fixed."

She disconnected the truck and drove into Chama and was back within an hour, followed by a man in a battered black truck who changed the huge tire and cut off the exhaust pipe while Linda chatted gaily and offered cash in exchange for charging a lower fee.

She was also a pro at bargaining and wanted to help if she thought I had been cheated. We came home from one trip to find my old Toyota totaled.

"A guy slammed right into me against a red light," my apologetic house sitter explained.

Linda turned to me. "I's coming with you to buy a new car so you get the best deal."

After the negotiations, she left me to complete the paperwork while she test drove a truck. Later, she demanded, "Let's see the papers" and spotted a new addition. "I's going back there to get your money back," she screamed. At the showroom, she accosted the salesman. "He wanted to continue in private, and I says, 'No, you's writing a check for me right here.'"

She returned in triumph, waving the check. "I saved you hundreds of dollars, babe. You need to have me look at stuff when you want to buy anything." I kissed my vociferous lover as she said with pride, "Leave it to me, babe; you's the professor."

Sometimes when Linda was staying with me, John came for dinner, bumping up the rocky driveway on his motorcycle in his leathers, with Wookie held on a cushion attached to the gas tank. John relaxed back in a chair, at ease in old khaki shorts and T-shirt, and Linda told him of my faulty washer.

After looking, he said, "I can fix that. I think it needs a new control board."

"That would be great, John."

He wrote down the model and serial number. "I'll bring the board next time."

Another time, when I was alone, bold Bowtie burst through the screen of the laundry door to follow a javelina. I was frantic. I called Linda, and she called John: "You gotta come and help us find Bowtie; he got out."

After an hour of searching with us, John declared, "I gotta go. Not sure what they'll say when I tell them at work that I was looking for the lost cat of my wife's lesbian lover!"

LINDA SPENT HALF HER time with John at the resort. They worked on their cars and played golf. They shopped for clothes and ate at Tex-Mex restaurants. She told me, "We usually share a plate cos two's more'n we want. I jokes to the waiter, 'He's too mean to buy two plates.'" After telling me this, she frowned. "I's guilty when I's with you cos I leave John alone and guilty when I's with John cos I leave you alone." Her situation was more complicated than mine. Sooner or later, it would surely be too stressful.

We had been together four years, and I pondered the dichotomy in my life. When she left my place for time with John, I did miss her. But solitude was nonetheless important for my reflective life. I found it gratifying how, in the quietude, the process of writing crystalized my thoughts. Vivian Gornick, in *The Romance of American Communism*, captured my feelings when she wrote, "The reason the work comes first in the case of the artist, the scientist, the thinker is that its practice makes flare into bright life a sense of inner expressiveness that is incomparable."* I realized there was a creative link between my exciting scientific endeavor and my new love of writing.

MY PART-TIME LIFE WITH Linda was filled with much that was novel and strange. But I loved being engaged in helping her be a wildlife enthusiast.

"Look, babe. How about this shot I got of a Gila woodpecker hanging upside down as it pokes its beak into the feeder?"

"Terrific. You got the angle just right." I smiled. "And, look, verdins hang upside down and get the drips underneath."

"And them red house finches can get tiny sips with their fat beaks from full feeders."

We watched bossy brown thrashers, loud-mouthed woodpeckers, and a pair of chirping cardinals that came into the big mesquite tree on my patio. Linda looked at all the birds with her new binoculars and felt a sense of pride that she had also found a reason to take up serious photography once more.

Inside my house, she investigated the contents of all my cupboards. Reaching up to a tattered old computer box, she found a collection of mammalian skulls. "What's these?"

"You can see they're skulls."

"Fuck, babe, they's all different."

As she gazed, I pointed out how the coyote had big canine teeth for tearing into flesh, and complex molars, while

---

* Vivian Gornick, *The Romance of American Communism*, 2020 edition, published by Verso.

the rabbit had chopping front teeth and grinding molars at the back.

"Cool," she responded. "They's so amazing."

"You can have them."

She picked up the different species, turning them over to examine their teeth and guess what they would have eaten, and I felt the joy of being a teacher who can unpack information that engenders interest. Decades earlier in England, I discovered that enchantment, unlocking the natural curiosity of high-school students to the marvels of biology.

Linda gleefully found a dead fox near the resort and got John to pick up the stinking thing, put it in a covered bucket, and take it home. Later, she brought it to my place. We laid it out on the ground and tried to hack off the head with an axe.

"Too leathery, eh?"

"Yes, bub, let's just bury the whole thing. All the bacteria and worms and things will eat out the flesh and leave the bones clean."

"And then we dig it up?"

"Exactly."

Linda dug a hole with my old pick and spade, and I kicked the corpse in and covered it, to be unearthed months later. I found a dusty glass-fronted case, and Linda arranged her skulls in order of size. She smiled as she meticulously cleaned the glass. "I's gonna have a museum!"

One day, we discovered a dead coyote lying by the sliding glass door to my bedroom.

"Babe, he's gorgeous, but how'd he die? He looks perfect. Let's pull that sucker out into the desert so he will rot away, and I can have a whole skeleton."

I thought, *Oh, dear.* There was no way we could put together 320 bones. I had unsuccessfully tried to put together a dingo skeleton in my college days but didn't want to dampen her enthusiasm. We left it by a tall saguaro away from the house, and every time she came from the resort, she rushed out: "Let's go see our rotting boy," and we went out through creosotes, prickly pear, and bursage. First it swelled a little, and I poked a hole in its taut skin with a stick, revealing a mass of maggots. "Oh, wonderful! Look at how the body is being cleaned up."

She screwed up her nose and covered her mouth with her hand, looking sideways at the seething mass. "Gross, but I know how you love that shit."

In time, maggots, beetles, vultures, and other scavengers exposed the skeleton and cleaned all the bones. But we got a shock later. "Holy shit, they's been half taken. Must be sum-bitch stoled them."

She suggested, "I's seen on TV that elephants scatter bones of dead relatives. Maybe coyotes do that." The lost bones thankfully curtailed the plan of building a standing skeleton, but she kept the skull.

DURING HER TIME AT the resort, Linda learned to play poker online while John was at work, and then came the casino. She was often radiant with pleasure when she came to my place. "Babe, I played twelve hours straight and won a ton a' money." She needed novelty. While I was pleased for her to have this diversion, I also provided anything that could engage her in discussion of biology, especially with the birds and bones but ultimately with all of nature.

APART FROM BAILEY THE Labrador and Wookie the Yorkie, Linda and John had two parrots—a Hahn's macaw and an African gray. "You should see them showering with me or throwing food and talking. They's such characters." I told her I once had space on campus in the same building as Irene Pepperberg, who owned the famously accomplished African gray, Alex.

"What a pest that bird was. Irene's students took him on walks, and I suffered the ear-splitting screeches as they wandered up and down the corridor outside my office."

Linda was thrilled. She knew all about Alex from TV. Among other abilities, he could name colors and correctly say the number of objects on a tray. Irene wrote that every night Alex would say, "You be good. I love you. See you tomorrow."

Soon after, Linda called from the resort. "Babe, can you look after our birds? I need to go to Vegas with John." I was reluctant but wanted to be helpful. I kept them at the far end of the house, where I would barely hear them. I was lucky not to have killed them after unknowingly replenishing their sunflower seeds with new ones that were salted, but their increased level of squawking alerted me in time. It took me almost a month to admit my mistake to Linda.

I ACCEPTED THAT JOHN was part of our lives and that Linda would spend time with him, so I felt free to engage in my own travels. In a visit to England, there was Jill, my close intellectual friend from Australia. "Bugger-lug," she called as she ran to me. It was a word we had picked up in Kent, where we both worked picking strawberries one long-ago summer, and Cockney women workers had called their little children by this curious endearment.

"Let's do Cornwall," I insisted. "Remember the youth hostels and how we hitchhiked all those narrow, twisted lanes edged with hedgerows and white-flowering cow parsley?"

We retraced our original route in a little red Nissan. At Tintagel Castle of King Arthur fame, we slipped on wet slate rocks and then rested on a bench outside the fourteenth-century post office building while willowy Jill, in hat with enormous brim, talked Queen Guinevere.

While still in Cornwall with our recollections, Jill announced, "We must clamber up Scarfell Pike in the Lake District and recite Wordsworth's 'I Wandered Lonely as a Cloud' when we get to the top."

Much of my time in England, though, was lost in memories of the Reg years, the soulmate time when I was younger. How we'd walk half a mile through leafy squares and along cobblestoned mews on the way to the lab as we held each other's gloved hands. On cold Saturdays, he'd say, "Let's have a blow," and we wandered in nearby Kensington Gardens. I wore my old maroon trench coat, while Reg wore an even older olive jacket and a tweed cloth cap torn in the back. A blustery wind blew in our faces as we watched boys with remote-controlled boats at the Round Pond, nannies wheeling babies under plane trees along Leicester Walk, or mothers playing with toddlers at the Peter Pan statue. In the evenings at the Cricketer's Arms, we drank pints of warm bitter. "We need to get tickets for Covent Garden; they're doing *The Tales of Hoffman*," he'd say with shining eyes.

Travels abroad with Linda were on a different level. They were not about my past; they were about seeing all that was new and enjoying her constant absorption of information. I could connect her with history and architecture as we wandered around Westminster Abbey in London, cultural diversity at the Papeete food truck park in French Polynesia, mammalian evolution in Australia. And there was always the excitement of new people with different customs: British, Irish, Fijian, Australian Aborigines. I loved the way she jumped up and down, took it all in, photographed everything. Texas ceased to be the center of her world.

Alone, I visited my sister, Jennifer, in Australia. "Bring me barbiturates from Mexico" she had begged when she had first recognized dementia coming, but I couldn't bring myself to do it. When I got there, I held her drooping hand in a yellow-painted sitting room where she sat with six other Alzheimer residents looking into space. Surprisingly, she was able to sing "The Foggy Dew" with me. In my childhood, she used to play it on the piano while I stood beside her, and our mother joined us in the singing. It was the last time she would recognize me, leading me to speculate on my own end. Reg and I had supported the idea of euthanasia, but as he came closer to death, he wanted to see that last sunset. I wondered if the same thing would happen to me, even though I was already prepared to be in control of my own ending. Linda agreed that being able to "die with dignity" was critical, but there was no way to tell if we would feel like that when the time came.

BACK AT MY HOUSE, I was ready for Linda. Her usual stream of verbiage brought me very much into the present: "You write for your bemusement. Tell me some antidotes," "You wanna make graphts outta all the circumfiction," "You so volumptuous," "Flick the nipplies," "muffin diving."

I introduced Linda to the "Trocks" (Les Ballets de Trockadero de Monte Carlo) with hairy male ballet dancers in all the female parts and dancing ever so slightly out of kilter with the music in *Les Sylphides*. It was hilarious as well as being top-quality ballet, and she hooted louder than anyone.

Linda discovered that David Sedaris was to visit. "We gotta go, babe; we love him."

And in that cavernous hall, he had the whole audience crying with laughter. I looked around at the gray-haired crowd and wondered if some of it was due to "inappropriate" sex jokes being not just funny but causing explosions because they were improper. After all, we cry with joy, laugh at disaster and awkwardness. Linda's jokes made me laugh because they were shocking as well as funny. That made her laugh, too, with gratification at her own ability.

We went to *Kinky Boots*, playing at Tucson Music Hall, a brutalist concrete building I knew well from operas and symphony concerts. When the performance ended, we found the main characters lingering in the foyer.

"There they are!" She handed me her phone. "Babe, quick, get a shot of me with them," and she ran up to all the red clothing and boots and flung her arms around two of the players. "Did ya get it? Did ya get it?" She didn't feel she had really been to an event or a place without the photos.

My gregarious lover especially enjoyed social events, and I liked to take her to neighborhood parties, where she made people laugh with her jokes. She was motivated by an audience that was more alive and mentally nimble than she had at the resort. At one BBQ, she hit it off so well with Rick that he lent us his motorcycle for an evening ride.

"Hold on tight, babe, we's gonna go like the wind on this motorsickle," she called, so excited to be riding as she had in her young days, with me, the novice, as pillion rider. Any new events or people made her laugh with pleasure. Not only was novelty special, but her need to surprise others with new jokes stemmed from the same thing.

I wondered how I could keep up with her need for newness. I must seem so prosaic and would surely become boring. I pondered what new entertainments I could provide and then had an idea: "How about going to Hawaii?"

"Oh, yes, babe." She rushed to the computer. "I'll pick the flights and seats. You figure out where to go when we's there."

As we circled several times over Honolulu, Linda frowned. "Something wrong, babe."

"Oh, I expect it's just busy." I put my arm around her.

"No, something wrong."

A voice came over the intercom: "We have no landing gear. Touchdown will be fast."

Linda glanced at me with pupils dilated and then glued her eyes to the window.

"The runway's lined with firetrucks!"

The sight of all that activity as we flashed in and then the bump of arrival on the tarmac seemed to stimulate more than frighten. The story of arriving in Hawaii was told for years.

Staying in quaint B&Bs as we drove around the Big Island was a novel experience for Linda, fascinated by thatched houses, quaint little bathrooms, windows with no blinds, new foods. "Them cinnamon malasada, babe! They's the best."

We stopped for a day at the Hawaii Tropical Bioreserve and Garden, among the Heliconia plants up and down steep green slopes. The leaves reminded me of banana plants, but the overwhelmingly extravagant red-and-yellow pendants of flowers were eye-catching.

"They's so big. Look at that sucker—whole hangy thing gotta be five feet long."

"Yes, amazing, but the real flowers are deep inside those crab claw bits." And I was gratified that she looked inside one of the huge bracts to see the flower.

We took our time. The carvings at Pu'uhonua o Hōnaunau National Historical Park looked down on us. The luminous green Waipio Valley and black solidified lava at Kilauea Iki

Crater at Volcano made me conscious of Hawaiian diversity. On Punalu'u black-sand beach, we saw domes of sleeping turtles, each too big to step over. "We need a selfie with them guys."

It was a carefree drive, with no fixed itinerary. Exploring a place together that was new to both of us increased our closeness. We ended with a week at a secluded rustic coffee shack, its many windows without glass and a hot tub hidden among trees. Here we watched emerald-green lizards flirting on banana leaves, listened to the squawking mynah birds and melodies from red-crested cardinals. We held each other's naked bodies as we watched an occasional silent yellow honeycreeper peep out from among coffee trees. Then we snorkeled and kayaked in nearby coral-rich Kealakekua Bay, where we also had to swim beside the kayak because: "Oh, babe, we's swimming with spinner dolphins!"

LINDA WAS RELAXED AWAY from the ambiguities of Tucson, and I knew she relished all the new things she was learning—the biology, the new places and cultures, and exactly who I was underneath a reserve that still surprised her. I was thrilled to provide knowledge and new horizons to a lover who had been deprived of what her clever, hyperactive mind craved. She was not the soulmate that Reg had been, with a closeness that barely needed words, but we shared a powerful togetherness.

I enjoyed both halves of my life. Being alone was rewarding for a deeper understanding of myself and others as I wrote this story in a peaceful desert paradise and took inspiration from the living world that flourished all around me. Life with Linda had given me an expanded appreciation of human difference. She was also the companion and jokester who brought me out of mourning. But more than that, I had a chance to share my life's good fortune with a new love and help to cultivate her uncommon abilities.

How long our strange arrangement would last was obscure. She could decide between John and me, or she could keep the half-time pattern. The choice would be hers. My past with Reg had been determinate, structured, targeted. With Linda, I lived in the unorganized present with an indefinite future, and I returned to a kind of passivity and acceptance that had provided a sanctuary in my underrated childhood. This time, it provided serenity when I might otherwise have been impatient with uncertainty.

14 A Village

ON A FIERY-HOT DAY in Tucson, Linda and I sat in the Arizona room as house finches panted in the draft of evaporative-cooler air exiting through the slightly open door. "We might could get a small cabin someplace cooler, eh?" Linda searched the mountains around Tucson on the computer and suddenly, "Found a place."

"What's it like?"

"No. Gotta go and see."

The next day, Linda took her truck, and I set off south in my car, winding through high desert grassland lush from recent rains. When I saw the drab half-finished cottage in Patagonia, I was disappointed. The realtor turned to me: "There's a bigger house just on the market. I'll take you just for the hell of it."

A dirt road up a short hill led to a secluded, three-acre mesa surrounded by washes. We parked in a mesquite bosque and walked along a path through a wooden arch. Laid out in front of us was a patio melded into a larger compound with a contorted mesquite tree and gardens dominated by the scarlet blooms of hummingbird trumpet bush, purple spikes of salvia, and yellow bells of *Tecoma*. On one side, a glass door led into the guest house, and beyond was an entrance to the main house. I looked south over a low wall past a mass of blue-flowering vitex shrubs shimmering with yellow swallowtail butterflies and a backdrop of oak-covered mountain wilderness extending to Mexico. Inside, I stared through each huge window: north through to Mount Wrightson, south to a garden patio, and a mesquite tree–filled enclosure. A room with three glass walls looked out on a fountain patio with white Ajo lilies just coming into flower.

The realtor explained, "It's architect-designed and entirely built of straw bales. You can see the walls are nearly three feet thick, and the glass room provides passive solar heating."

Within minutes, I *knew* I had to have it.

I turned to Linda. "Just look." I gasped.

I hadn't planned to live in Patagonia, but it felt magical, and it seemed that Linda could come at intervals just the same. She returned to Tucson, and I drove through the little town and luxuriant hills with my heart racing. I offered the full asking price.

It took a year to transfer my life. After Reg's death, it was time to move forward—to leave the home that embodied loss. I hadn't even considered Linda when buying my new house, but she seemed happy. "I's always wanted to live in a straw bale house. And all that land!" I also imagined I might be alone one day. A guest house would be there for a helper.

Before I moved, we revisited Patagonia. Wandering along the narrow park running through the village center, we watched red-and-blue buntings and a yellow hooded oriole hopping through the branches of Arizona walnut trees. Trains once chugged along here on their way from Benson to Guaymas, and an old semaphore signal remained. Old railway buildings held the history of local mining and ranching. At the 1930s Wagon Wheel Saloon, we ate chicken tacos at the bar. Linda was ecstatic. "Look at that old jukebox, and all them stuffed animals, and guns hanging from the ceiling. Love this place." From the Wagon Wheel, it would be a five-minute walk up the hill to the straw-bale house.

We poked our heads into the Stage Stop Inn with its vintage, glass-enclosed reception desk, and Linda photographed the floor tiles, each displaying an Arizona cattle brand. The marshal's office was fronted by a small windowless concrete structure with a sign on the front, "Patagonia Jail 1938." We watched a stream of dark-haired schoolchildren run into the general store across the street, and I reminded Linda that this southern strip of Arizona was only purchased from Mexico in 1853.

On the day of the move, Linda arrived with clothes, computer, and camera gear. The boxes of her past remained in the house she shared with John. We sat under a mesquite tree adorned with new, lime-green foliage, with clusters of pink penstemon flowers around us, and Mount Wrightson in the distance.

I breathed a sigh. "It's heaven!"

"Such a different life, eh, babe?" Linda savored details— so many new things. "Great, straw bale! Look how wide the windowsills are, perfect seats. Babe, we can have chickens and goats and a horse, grow our own stuff. We gonna do organic. Did you see they's made those raised beds in a big, fenced yard? We'll need a composter and a wormery. I saw fruit trees." She looked at me with eyebrows raised and eyes sparkling, and I felt a rush of affection, but I was again owning and organizing a home principally for myself.

As I put all my clothes in drawers and arranged my pictures on the walls, Linda roamed the village asking everyone, "Who are you?" She came home breathless.

"Hey, I met Saul. He makes cool art from thrown-out stuff, and he's married to Martha. She does pottery. Saul's funny, and he's got a work shed made of old theater props cos that was his job. Pat's a lesbian and plays flute in your orchestra—you know, Tucson symphony shit. She introduced me to Metal Joe. He's small and shuffly, but his metal art is good."

We became friends with all these characters as Linda enabled me to assimilate into the life of the township sooner than I would have done by myself.

Not long after we arrived, we were at our computers when the power went off.

"Fuck," shouted Linda. "No water either because of the well pump."

We went down to the post office, where we found the expected throng.

"How long might it last?" I asked.

"Oh, could be hours. Or days. This is our town. Yeah, not part of your perfect modern life."

IN THE GARDEN ENCLOSURE, we worked to dig out straggly weeds and turn soil in the old, raised beds. Linda dressed up for it—work shirt, overalls, and boots. She dug energetically with the spade: "Shitty deep roots. Mom used to grow okra. Can we have okra?"

When our wriggling worms came in the mail, Linda poked around in the sawdust with a stick. "Gonna count them all, babe, to make sure we's not cheated."

On the side of one of the beds, we separated worms for the garden and the wormery. We were just a few short of the hundred. "Guess that's okay then."

She spent a few days each week with me but often remarked, "I can never leave John." He was a regular visitor, always friendly to me. Working to divide the large mesquite enclosure into a dog run and a chicken yard, he asked, "What do you think, Liz?" I watched him, a large man in old clothes, with straggly light-brown hair and beard framing a plain face. How tolerant he seemed. How lonely he must be. I felt for this shy man, who seemed to lack comrades and needed to be friends with me to be close to Linda.

Meanwhile, Linda had plenty of ideas: "Want them spotty chickens, eh?"

"Yes, Barred Rocks. We must build them a coop."

"Oh, babe, yes. Let's make it out of bottles! We can go dumpster-diving for wine bottles at the recycling place. I saw it behind the post office."

We made a wood frame with a metal roof and made trips down the hill for bottles. Linda took the lead. "Let's have clear glass ones for the north wall. They's gotta have a nice north light for artwork." I laughed. "We could put the clear ones on the south side to confuse them."

We watched the Barred Rocks, White Leghorns, and tiny Silkies as they grew. We learned their individual personalities and waited for eggs. Linda's work on the bottle job slowed down after a few months, and I continued the work myself. I was not surprised really, but when would she get bored with me too?

Having a garden took me back to my Queensland childhood. Mother and I worked together in the garden when I came home from school. We grew love-in-a-mist and delphiniums because blue was her favorite color, as she told me about how bees pollinated the flowers. Later, I realized this was her attempt to tell me about reproduction. But it was there with my devoted mother that my love of plants took root, and the hours of kneeling together and talking were never long enough. In Patagonia, alone with my trowel among the vegetables, I was back to the close companionship of our gardening in those long-ago Brisbane days, while Linda put netting over the large chicken run to foil the hawks.

It remained a battle to keep out predators. Coatimundi and coyotes climbed over the top, and foxes dug under the fence. A lot more wire netting had to be employed. We learned from our neighbor, Dick, that our decapitated birds resulted from spotted skunks squeezing through the cyclone fence at night and attacking chickens on their roost. Once, two rattlesnakes got caught in the netting that supplemented the fence around the chicken run.

"Fuck! Rattlers," Linda shouted and rushed down the hill to Dick, who came up to help extricate them. "Nice specimens you got here," as he chopped their heads off. He later brought us a perfectly prepared rattlesnake skin, and Linda declared, "You ain't hanging that in the house!"

I placed rocks and plantings of blue salvia around the edge of a new pond we made outside the living room, and from our armchairs, we saw javelinas trotting up from below and cottontail rabbits warily hopping to the new watering place. Then came the birds. Mourning doves usually came in pairs, but green-tailed towhees ran up for a quick sip, and redheaded house finches descended from the overhanging mesquite branches. I could watch for hours, but ten minutes was enough for Linda.

Each day, we made the round trip down the hill with Bailey and along the main street to the post office. "Hello. You visiting?" Linda asked when we passed a group sitting outside the Gathering Grounds coffee shop. If they were walkers on the Arizona Trail, carrying huge backpacks, Linda shouted, "Great walking. Wouldn't wanta be ya."

If we stopped to buy ice cream or coffee, we sometimes sat with Pat the flutist. She was also a major hiker and cyclist. Her very tanned, lined face readily broke into a smile. One day, two very slender women in white baggy pants and long-sleeved white tops came in. Pat leaned over to whisper, "You guys watch them."

They bought chocolate brownies. Pat laughed. "They're patrons at the Tree of Life and wear white for purity. They pay a fortune there to eat nothing, but they come into town to sneak cookies. It's supposed to be a rehab center, but rich people come from all over for health and so-called spiritual programs. Some patrons end up staying in town and building fancy houses."

Birders were conspicuous with their floppy hats and binocular harnesses. Linda was always ready with advice: "You gotta go to the lake if you want to see trogons. And they's the Nature Conservancy just down the road." When competitive birders wanting to add to their list (listers) came for a sighting of a rare plain-capped starthroat hummingbird that had just been recorded there, she told them, "Go to Patten's place to see them suckers."

The post office was the major hub. "Hi," Linda called as she pet a dog, struck up a conversation about local news, or told people all about herself. Sometimes it was, "Who the hell are you?" And so would begin a new friendship with Ann, or Cici, or Annette. As we learned later, Annette had a little dog who got his back end cleaned with a tissue whenever he did his business. "Look, babe, there goes the butthole-wiping lady."

Linda figured out when everyone visited the post office to pick up their mail. If you wanted to see Marge, you went at ten, George at ten thirty, Phyllis at three—and never mind trying to bump into Pauline, who went at night to avoid seeing anyone. We often met Ann Swan there, an elderly widow who was always ready with quips about other people that totally matched Linda's. She was a well-known fabric artist and had showed at major galleries in Chicago, but in retirement, she had become one of the characters in Patagonia, radiating a kind of who-cares-about-anything manner.

"Where do people get pot here?" Linda asked her.

"You go out in the street and call, 'I want pot,' and people will come running." She laughed loudly, making everyone in the vicinity smile.

WE HUNG BIRD FEEDERS on our patio and scanned the hills and washes around the house with our binoculars. Linda was the first to spot a new bird; I was the one with the patience to watch it.

"Make a spreadsheet," she demanded.

It was Linda who wrote down Western tanagers. "Hey, babe, these red-and-yellow guys snap up honeybees on the flowers of that tree. Why don't they get bit?"

"Oh, yes, that's an eastern locust tree. I got the yellow-and-black orioles on our pears."

Blue grosbeaks unexpectedly nested in our patio mesquite. Rufous hummingbirds showed up in April going north and then in August going south. The final species list nudged one hundred.

"Might could get good shots," Linda shouted, setting up a remote control so that she could sit indoors and photograph birds without disturbing them. The stunning closeups of a dozen species told us more about them, like the one of a blue grosbeak with a beak full of grasshoppers—a versatile seedeater could switch to other foods that were more abundant.

"Gonna get the pictures in that gallery down on the main street."

Photography was not just about Linda's enhanced interest in birds. We installed trail cameras all around the property to capture wildlife. Each morning, "Hurry, babe, get the camera cards. Gotta see who's come in the night." Linda didn't want to possibly encounter a rattlesnake. We sat together at my computer—colored pictures in the daytime, ghostly black and white infrared photos of coyotes, raccoons, and rodents at night, often looking blankly into the camera. We got one photo of a hog-nosed skunk on the black icy pond, its tall, airy tail hiding the rest of its body, the round patch of skin of its anus highlighted in the flash.

"A great shot of an asshole," Linda declared.

JOHN OFTEN STAYED IN the guest house on weekends, and he helped Linda set up matting and framing equipment while I settled to write until she suddenly saw some new bird or had a sudden idea. "I know you's working, but listen to this. I'm gonna have my own show! I gotta go round and tell everyone to come."

We joined the library. "Hi, Abbie," we greeted the reticent head librarian with waist-length white hair and baggy gray pants.

She smiled, looking down. "You girls settled in now?"

The building had been a hotel in 1910. A series of small rooms opening onto a long corridor with computers was complemented by a large reading room and another for community events. A notice board listed a reading by Robin Kimmerer, author of *Braiding Sweet Grass*, and a field day of identifying animal footprints, run by Jessica Lamberton, a biologist at Sky Island Alliance. With our library cards in hand, Abbie told us dogs were allowed, and instead of fines, late-book offenders had to leave food for the poorest in town.

ON OUR TOURS THROUGH town, Linda talked to visitors with particular enthusiasm if their cars had a Texas plate. "Where're you from? Whatcha doing here?" The round-trip home went up another hill, past Charlee Farley's hair salon and Jill's blue mobile home, toward The Mesa gated properties, and then across a dam over a wilderness-filled canyon and back through the vegetable-garden enclosure to the house.

One day, notices went up at the post office for one of Patagonia's many famous parties where Hawaiian shirts and leis flew wildly to the music of the local Hog Canyon Band. "Look over there," Linda said, pointing to the craziest dancing we had ever seen. Some had rhythm, others had the strangest hops and arm thrusts, but the most amazing dancer was a very tall artist, Helen. She danced by herself: long legs kicking high, skirt swirling, arms making circles, all in one smooth continuous movement. Eventually, we joined in.

South of Patagonia is the vast prairie of San Rafael Valley, where *Oklahoma!* was filmed. There, at monthly potluck parties, we watched a red sun sink below the western hills while the full moon came up over the Huachuca mountains and silvered the wide, empty prairie. In awed silence, we ate quiche and salad and cake spread out on collapsible tables.

Linda and I became workers and naturalists together. For the first time since college days, I enjoyed crazy parties. And so, in the contented fullness of our lives, my rich past with Reg was consigned to a deeper memory.

I DID WELCOME MY days of solitude when Linda was in Tucson, and I often watched life at the pond. White-tailed deer tiptoed up from the valley and nervously approached the water on slender legs, drinking deeply before scavenging for seeds spilled from a bird feeder. They balanced on hind legs to reach up to the feeder, where their tongues extracted seeds, and then ran back down the hill with white flags of tails held high.

By midmorning, Gambel's quail foraged for seeds on the ground, along with different kinds of sparrows. A curve-billed thrasher would race out from the yucca, pick up a few seeds, run at the sparrows, scatter the quail, and then rush back into shelter. So bossy and bad-tempered. Doves came and stood side by side, their synchronized sips spreading interlocking sets of ripples. They flew off when a green-tailed towhee landed too close. It drank briefly and returned to its curious digging dance, two feet dragging the soil back, then a small jump, and both feet repeating the coordinated scratch.

One morning, seven javelinas pranced along on their tiny high heels. The buff adults came straight to the pond, while the youngsters snuffled in the dry grass before running to nuzzle the others. But after five minutes, they wandered off, over the edge of the mesa. I became addicted to this scene, its ever-changing light, reflections of the mesquite tree and salvia bushes on the water, the old branching yucca and spreading alligator juniper beyond, the parade of birds, Mount Wrightson in the distance. I imagined being old and alone, reflecting on the past as I watched the soothing busyness.

We had many visitors in that first year. Friends came, of course, curious to see the home that had enchanted us or eager to take part in one of the many festivals. Former colleagues and students came from around the world, but when six entomologists came, led by Dave, a former student from my Berkeley days and now a professor in Connecticut, we had the most fun. We helped for several diligent weeks as they collected and reared caterpillars, feeding individuals all through the night, photographing the species for Dave's coming book on caterpillars of the Southwest.

We made friends with Emily, the Happy Cookers caterer, who looked vaguely Native American. Her Labrador, Chaco, was the son of a pair of black labs that had provided a dozen others for the village. We had been in Patagonia less than a year when a new litter arrived.

"Hey, babe, a puppy would help Bailey; she so depressed."

"Cute, but we can't have one—too much work."

Six weeks later, when Linda was in Tucson, I went to see the puppies that were ready to be adopted. I picked up a little boy. He licked my hand and cuddled up to me.

I called Linda. "Bailey would love to have a puppy after all. We need a puppy."

"No, we don't. Do we really?"

"Bailey says she wants a puppy."

"Fuck, get the damn thing."

Linda came rushing back to Patagonia and fell for the puppy, of course. After two sleepless nights of puppy crying, I sighed. "I can't do it. I just can't manage without sleep."

"Yeah, I's dead."

The owners were accommodating as I handed him back, tears rolling down my cheeks.

For two whole days, Linda lay in bed and cried. "I loved that puppy. Bailey needs a puppy. Puppy! Puppy! I want a puppy."

I went back and retrieved the puppy. We converted a shed into a doggie apartment with a door to the dog run, and there, Bailey taught little Bandit good behavior. He was also best friends with his brother Chaco, and he became the most beloved of dogs in the whole village.

Jill asked Linda in her very English accent, "How did you decide on the name Bandit?"

"Because he stoled our hearts."

In each other's embrace, we didn't need to express delight in our new life, and Linda's visits became longer until she was with me full time. I accepted that, just as I had earlier accepted her choices of when to come and go. Linda was a free spirit and hard to pin down. An attempt to formalize anything could backfire, so I chose to preserve the status quo without comment. She told me later she had thought, *What if she throws me out for just staying without being invited?*

I would be giving up all the peaceful days of solitude that had restored so much to my despairing spirits, but I would have a lover and companion whose vigorous mind and ingenuities foiled melancholy. I thought about her short attention span and love of novelties. Would she tire of me and of Patagonia? Would John finally detach himself from Linda now that she and I lived together full time, or would he always be a presence? Linda had said she couldn't leave John out of her life, and he seemed content with our crazy triangle. We had drifted into an unknown landscape, and I would have to wait.

15 Genetic Trail

"WONDER IF DOROTHY IS dead yet." Linda's question took me by surprise. She had told me about Dorothy, her birth mother, who had sold her many offspring from different fathers. Linda felt lucky to have been adopted at birth by a kind older couple who repeatedly told her, "You're God's gift to us." She dumped a box of papers on the dining table from her first research on Dorothy. "See what you can make of it all."

There were two birth certificates. The original was signed by the mother as Dorothy Hoeflein. Linda was called "baby girl," and the box for "illegitimate" was checked. The second was made for her adoption, with her new name, Linda Christine Hitchcock.

I found certificates of marriages, divorces, and births; a string of fraud felony charges of Dorothy's; and some mug shots of half-brothers. Friendly letters from a Linda Hoeflein were intriguing. "Who is she?"

"We think we's half-sisters with a shared father. We's both adopted."

"How about a DNA test?"

"Really? That would be amazing."

The results showed they were unrelated, which was a

bitter disappointment for both Lindas. More extraordinary was that Linda had a full brother in England with a probability of 99.9 percent. Paul was a successful business consultant, seventeen years younger, with a wife and two children. The two of them talked on FaceTime. He seemed charming, accomplished, and fun. Suddenly, all she had believed for twenty-five years about a terrible family was eclipsed by Paul.

"Do we look alike?" she kept asking me.

I smiled. "Maybe."

"How did you get to England?" she asked Paul.

"Well, I think I was adopted. A DNA test did show that my brother is not my real brother. That's all I know—my mother won't talk. She worked near an American base in Scotland where there was a home for unwanted babies, so perhaps she got me there."

Paul was a major contrast with the drug addicts and convicts among the half-siblings she had tracked down earlier. Here was comforting evidence that nurture mattered more than nature. Her adoptive parents were dead, but she hoped their influence impacted her more than whatever she may have inherited from Dorothy. Her excitement was infectious, and I was anxious to discover more myself. We had to meet Paul.

Revisiting England with Linda was exciting for me too—the country had been my second home for years. It was where I had become a scientist and fallen in love.

"We's coming to visit," Linda told him. She put her arms around me tightly and her head on my chest. "Babe, a full brother and so nice!"

By the time we left Arizona, Linda felt she knew Paul and his family from hours on FaceTime. Gliding over the Atlantic, I held her sticky hand as we descended to green southern

England. We checked into the Beaufort, a boutique hotel occupying a large Georgian townhouse in Knightsbridge. The elegant building was one of similar grand houses around leafy Beaufort gardens and a good start for introducing Linda to the charms of London. Arriving in the afternoon, we relaxed after the long journey with a cream tea—scones, strawberry jam, and clotted cream—as we looked out into the elm-green square from our small room.

Paul was to visit us after work in London the following day. As the time approached, Linda became restless. "Let's go out and meet him."

We walked to the street corner near the tube station and waited. Suddenly, there he was—a tall, good-looking man striding down Brompton Road in a long black overcoat.

"Paul," Linda called, and he turned to face us. For a moment, they just looked before racing to each other for a big hug.

In our hotel room, the three of us scrutinized the data splayed over the coffee table. As Paul puzzled over the figures, Linda and I took in more of his round open face, his polite British manners and speech, his wide smile and mousy hair. But after a couple of hours, he left to catch a commuter train to Sevenoaks in Kent. "I need to get home for the kids, but I'll be in touch."

A couple of days later, we met the family in their home. Blond, smiling Susan and two bouncy children welcomed us with hugs. Linda laughed as she looked fondly at Paul. "I got actual family now."

Susan was totally engaged. "Just think: two people on different sides of the Atlantic mysteriously brother and sister!"

"So hard to imagine how a baby here came from America."

I looked at Paul's big head and wide smile and Linda's

small head and faint dimples. They didn't look alike, but I felt a glow of joy in Linda's excitement.

Linda had a birthday during the time we were in England. Paul and Susan put on a birthday tea and showered her with presents: Scottish shortbread, English chocolates, a book about Kent, and a variety of British-themed knickknacks. The children gave her handmade birthday cards. We sat in their conservatory looking out onto a grassy backyard as we drank our tea and Paul cut the cake. I watched Linda—so happy at an English birthday tea. Susan was most fascinated by how baby Paul had ended up in England. "Such a mystery, and Dorothy doesn't sound like a traveler."

Paul was exuberant. "I'm American!" he shouted with excitement and jumped up out of his chair with one long arm reaching up to the top of the doorway. "I'm going to come over to Texas and eat barbecue!" Little Rachel and Mark ran around the table, laughing. "We're coming too!"

Later, we strolled around nearby Ightham Mote, a medieval moated manor house and gardens in Kent, not much changed since it was built in the fourteenth century. I was fascinated, but Linda was focused on family. We loitered in the gardens. The gentle English sunny day among the masses of lavender and blue campanulas, red and white sweet Williams, and pink Dianthus made for a relaxing place to consider the mysteries.

At the end of our visit, any sadness in our goodbyes to them all was offset by general excitement, ideas for future visits, and the research ahead. Looking out at emerald England from the return train to London took me back decades. In my youth, I had reveled in the scenes I had pictured from English literature studied during my Australian childhood. And I had met a cousin—my father's sister married an Englishman before I was born. The family lived close to where Paul now lived. How often on weekends I had taken this train to stay in a little converted oasthouse surrounded by farmland on the chalk hills of southern England.

BACK HOME IN ARIZONA, Linda kept in touch with Paul on FaceTime. She sent him a tie with a DNA motif for his birthday. Paul wanted another DNA test to be sure, and the second set of results came in with an even higher probability of Linda and Paul being full siblings. Internet research began in earnest. There were even more marriages, divorces, births, and criminal activity associated with Dorothy. Some of the twenty-two children had been born before she married anyone, and for part of the time in her thirties and forties, she was married to two men concurrently—Norbert deLory and Willie Britt. The marriage to Norbert covered the birth dates of both Linda and Paul. Was he their father? Research showed no evidence of children, and the idea of Norbert as father faded.

The precise date of Paul's birth could not be established from his apparently fake Scottish birth certificate, and we couldn't find a record of his actual birth in the United States. Where had Paul been born? Who was their father? Linda talked on the phone to Dorothy's stepsister in North Carolina.

"Dorothy visited back over here when she were twenty-seven after leaving William Hoeflein, and she and Willie Britt got together, and Willie just a teenager. That were before you was born. She went for the young boys, but she did finally marry Willie."

Suddenly it seemed that Willie could be the father of both Linda and Paul.

"Dorothy were always pregnant. All them babies, always dumped them, never mind the abortions. I remember when she come over here with the baby she called Booboo, and I put her on a train, and when she come back a few days later, she no longer had Booboo. You might never know who your daddy was—Dorothy run off with every man she could."

The more we found out, the more sordid Dorothy's life sounded, and the more appalled Linda became. But it did seem possible that Dorothy became pregnant from a relationship with Willie, making him Linda's father though they were not yet married.

Dorothy's sister knew more. On the phone, Linda asked, "Do you know which kid she called Booboo?"

"Honey, she called ever' one Booboo before she got rid a' them. She were bad-tempered—she got a drink in her and turned nasty. I haven't seen Dorothy for twenty year and don' know nothing about her now, but she were bad. There was one time when she went off with some man and left two kids at home. Well, they had a car accident, and I says to her when she got back, 'You wouldn'a had a problem if you hadn't been giving him head.'"

Willie and Dorothy were divorced a few years after Paul would have been born, lending support to the possibility that Willie was the father of them both, though no records could be found of children born to Dorothy after Linda's birth in 1955. Linda eventually tracked down where Dorothy lived in a small Texas town. Surely, at this stage of her life, she would tell us what we so badly wanted to know.

Linda scowled, holding back tears. "There's no way I can talk to her."

For me it was easier—I had none of the burden of the "the primal wound" of being taken from one's birth mother and none of the emotions engendered by having an abusive, abandoning one. I called Dorothy, and some stories agreed with what we knew. It was time to go further.

"Well, you had a daughter in 1955 who was adopted at birth," I pressed.

"No, I never," she insisted as she rambled on about Willie and Norbert, two men we knew she was married to at the same time.

"What about a son in 1972?" I asked.

"They's no other children. I know cos they's not written in my Bible. An' I don't care what anyone says. I were never a whore or a bigamist, and I got nothing to tell you."

Linda cried as she laid her head on my lap. "She got rid a' me, and now she don't even let me exist!"

I stroked her short, graying hair, but there was nothing I could say to console her. It was hard to imagine how I would feel in her place.

A year later, Dorothy's death closed the door to finding out more from her but led to more details about her on the internet. At least eleven marriages, including three concurrent when she was eighteen. Never mind common-law marriages. But no birth certificate for Paul.

Linda and Paul both felt Willie must be their father, though the mystery remained of where and when Paul was born, how he got across the Atlantic, and where his adoptive mother had found him.

I pondered the improbabilities and researched DNA tests. Both tests had used the same limited set of markers. Sharing none of them would clearly indicate no relationship, but sharing most of them could occasionally happen by chance. A DNA test of the wider genome would offer certainty. We chose 23andMe. The results were devastating; they were not related at all!

"Two out of three, babe," Linda cried, not wanting to believe the importance of the more comprehensive 23andMe tests.

Paul began to back off visiting the United States. Face-Time and emails faded away.

"Paul's gone," Linda cried as I hugged her.

"Paul dumped me," she told people as she burst into tears.

Linda felt the intensity of rejection. Her birth mother had sold and given away children, denied Linda's existence, and now the promised brother had evaporated. She put away the reams of papers and the photos and no longer searched for documents. Six months after Paul's last contact he sent a final email, explaining that Y chromosome tests had definitively shown him to be the sone of a man his mother had been secretly seeing at the relevant time.

All the thrill of finding Paul and developing affection for him as an impressive brother with a happy family was ended. I looked at her tearful face and felt an agony of remorse. "I am so sorry I even suggested DNA tests," I muttered.

She cried as she replied, "Now I have no one."

No one? She knew well enough that I was there for her, but disappointment about Paul consumed her emotions at this distressing time. The "no one" was a measure of her grief.

Meanwhile, DNA databases continued to list more genetic relatives—mostly distant Cajun cousins. Dorothy was from North Carolina, so Linda's genetic father had to be Cajun. Linda commented, "It'd only take a one-night stand."

We took a motor home trip to Texas and Louisiana, hoping to find out more. First, we visited the Rosenberg Library in Galveston. At the history center in the grand 1904 Renaissance building, librarians helped us find the address of the shoe shop where Linda's parents worked at the time they adopted her. We also found the approximate address of the Imperial Club, a bar nearby where her birth mother, Dorothy, worked during the same period. The shoe shop was still there, converted to an art gallery. The Imperial Club in the adjacent block was gone.

It seemed likely that Linda's adoptive parents-to-be would have known Dorothy; her father was a man who liked a beer after work and probably drank at the nearby club. An adoption arrangement could even have been made during Dorothy's pregnancy.

Linda was dejected. "What mother would sell her babies? And what kind of person is going to buy small children in a bar?"

I knew that so much shocking information and feelings of loss had a profound effect on her and felt wretched that the likelihood of ever finding a father was close to zero. As someone who knew her own long family history, I couldn't put myself in Linda's place. Was I too self-confident because of my privileged background? Was I blasé about my mother's insistence that our forebears were special? I lacked the wounds that might result from having been abandoned or from the feeling of inheriting bad characteristics. My mother had a fixation about bad genes and loved to tell us children that we had good genes. Linda knows scientific study now indicates that as much as 50 percent of our behavioral and personality traits are inherited. She wondered what awful traits she might share with Dorothy.

We had some good interludes on our trip, though—long walks on Galveston beach, where we camped in the motor home, and rambles through the historic streets lined with Victorian houses, their fresh multicolored paint enhancing fancy woodwork. One had been converted into a cozy restaurant, where we sat wondering about the events of 1954 and who slept with Dorothy on that fateful August night.

We traveled on to southern Louisiana, where most of

the DNA-linked relatives lived, before realizing how complicated it would be to find a particular man from so long ago. In Lafayette, we picked up a phone book to look up people with the surnames listed as Linda's possible links on Ancestry.com. A man hearing Linda's story said, "Honey, any them names you look up will have dozens a' pages in that book."

We stayed in campgrounds where people lived in rundown trailers. Men sat outside smoking while barefoot children stood in doorways. When we passed a toothless old man in the street, Linda said with a phony laugh, "Might be me dad, eh?"

I wondered about putting a notice in the Lafayette newspaper: "Anyone have a relative who was in Galveston in August 1954?" We never did it. Who would want to tell strangers that a relative had an affair in Texas, and how reasonable was it to even ask?

A boat trip down the Bayou Teche gave us a break from thinking about relatives in Louisiana as we were taken into the great Atchafalaya swamp. So many bald cypress trees, their fall foliage dark orange, and all of them draped in pale-green Spanish moss. Scattered among them were small Cajun houses, some on islands, some on rafts. The guide took us through a maze of waterways with messy beaver dens and alligators peeping out of the water. There must have been plenty of life in the water with all the poised herons and egrets, blue kingfishers, and bald eagles, all of them eyeing the water for movement. Linda waxed ecstatic. "Babe this place is the best. This is real Cajun country. Gotta be a ton a' crawdads. I love them crawdads."

Interestingly, Linda's adoptive mother was full Cajun and cooked gumbo and jambalaya, but the crawdads, or freshwater crayfish, were her favorites.

Many adoptees ache to know about their genetic relatives,

and the feeling seems to be part of knowing oneself, even if searches lead to the disillusion of finding birth parents who seem uncaring. How important was it to me to know that I inherited my mother's spotted eyes, my father's wavy hair, my grandfather's curiosity? Did it matter that my forbears were well-regarded citizens in Australian history? I had always taken my ancestry for granted. I can't judge how much the knowledge has shaped me, but it made me feel special as a child, which in turn probably helped to give me confidence. Linda's excitement over Paul had ended in bereavement, and we were getting nowhere with finding her father. I felt that her concern about forebears in some way gave her an insecurity that had played out even in our relationship.

Back in Arizona, Linda sat at her computer. "Got another LeBlanc cousin!" One sent an extensive LeBlanc family tree. Then came a couple of close DNA matches on a branch of that tree, indicating Linda had to be on the tree. A genealogist identified her paternal great-grandparents as Andre Lucius LeBlanc and Felicienne Thibodeaux. One of their three sons must be her grandfather. Linda contacted various descendants, some of whom offered to take DNA tests.

Linda spent bouts of time looking through newspaper archives with obituaries, contacting possible half-siblings or their children, trying to get help from more distant genetic relatives who lived in or near Lafayette. We complemented each other in the search. She went down every path writing copious notes and was sidetracked into how she might be related to a hundred other distant cousins. I focused on who her father was. After ten years of searching, all the data led definitively to Ray Joseph LeBlanc, who had to be her father. Now we had the answer. Ray Joseph was the unusual Cajun who left his neighborhood and moved to Texas, where he worked on boats, sometimes berthed in Galveston. One cousin simply said he was a "character," but we found few records, and he had no recorded children with his wife. The one photo Linda obtained of Ray Joseph from the web was taken when he was obviously quite old, but there is a clear likeness.

It was important to Linda to find her exact place in the genetic tree, to discover who slept with Dorothy that August of 1954. She had loved her adoptive parents, and her need didn't relate to a deprivation of not having had close parental bonds. Nor did she think much about inherited health factors. It was not about wanting a context for her life that felt lacking, though she would have been thrilled to find someone she looked like. She most needed to know her paternal genetic heritage because she hoped to see somebody she could respect, to counteract the thought of a mother she could only detest. But we will never know what her genetic father was like or what features Linda may have inherited from him, and I think his living relatives have little interest in illegitimate offspring.

"Bub, I know it's disappointing, but those unknown people don't mean so much. I am the person who really cares about you. I love you."

Linda looked at me wistfully. "Babe, I loves you too, but I's always wanting to know about my baby-girl daddy."

16 Goodbye, Patagonia

IT WAS NOT SURPRISING that Linda's crazy jokes had been good for me; according to research by behavioral scientists, when a comical punch line hits, the brain's reward system lights up. And the desolation of Reg's dying days had changed to happy memories of all those good years. Linda and I had also grown into easy companions, together full time in Patagonia. We shoveled shit out of the chicken coop for the garden, pulled weeds, watched for the bobcat that had so enthralled us when he'd walked proudly by the water trough. I loved our daily walks through town and meeting visitors as Linda uncovered their interesting stories.

Once we encountered a tired-looking young man in tattered clothes with a monocycle.

"Where've you been?" called Linda.

"Oh, just come down the Continental Divide Trail."

"But it don't come through here."

"Well, I got to Deming in New Mexico and decided to make a detour to see a friend."

"Who's ya friend?"

He gave the name of a woman we knew, but he had no address or phone number. It was the kind of help that Linda delighted to give. She especially loved the interlude after discovering that the guy had done the whole trail on a mono-cycle twice. And on top of that, the "detour" from Deming was 220 miles!

Social events were part of our lives—but very different from the fancy dinner parties in the distant past with Reg. There was Jan's Garden, where we sat around a big picnic ta-ble under a huge, contorted mesquite tree. Everyone passed joints or bongs until we reeled into a concert at the Amish barn. New Year's Eve parties were legendary. The whole vil-lage drank and danced in historic Cady Hall at the library. Normally slow to join in, I hopped about to the sounds of a loud band and Linda's laugh. A Christmas at Paula's studio, where our small unkempt friend pulled out dozens of her paintings, had a different charm. Her quiet sense of humor undercut our shared reserve, and I felt a strong connection as she laughed awkwardly. I bought *The Penitent*, a rather ambig-uously cynical painting of a young man smoking. I have him on the wall—a rebel I can identify with.

On a day in September, the smell of browning short crust wafted through Patagonia, heralding the annual pie auction in aid of the community garden. Fifty pie boxes were piled up in the gazebo, tables and chairs laid out on the grass, and a grill readied for Emily's barbecue skills. We sat with Pat the flutist and her film editor partner, Michele, and several other friends, all of us hungry as Emily worked her magic. As the sun set, a voice came over the loudspeaker.

"Going, going, gone—Julie's chocolate cream pie for seventy-five dollars?" But I was waiting for Linda's favorite, a coconut pie.

Suddenly, "Best pie, baked by Cassina. Anyone more than a hundred dollars?"

I got it for a hundred and twenty. We all knew Cassina was the best baker, and as the others at the table shouted congratulations, Linda kissed me gently. "Thank you, babe." But eight tongues at our table were hanging out, and the pie was quickly reduced to crumbs.

We met Susan at a pie auction. Statuesque with wavy gray hair falling over her face, she was director of the Hummingbird Monitoring Network. She was not totally at ease but had a ready laugh, while her husband, Lee, of the neat beard and the sweetest smile, was silent. With them were interns from Mexico, Ecuador, and Bolivia. Linda and I fell for them all with their youthful enthusiasm for bird work and life in general.

"Let's have Rocio and Andrea an' them for supper."

"We can have them all to our place."

Soon I was helping to band hummingbirds, five hours every other week. Lee ran the catching operation at feeders set near his wildflower garden in the Patagonia Mountains. As a bird dipped its beak into the sugar water, he released a cord, and a cylindrical net curtain descended, enclosing both feeder and bird. A helper then reached up through the opening below, gently caught the hummingbird, and put it in a mesh bag. Susan gave the rest of us our jobs. We measured, weighed, and recorded significant features of each bird. Susan, peering through an Opti visor, bent the band onto a leg with tiny pliers handcrafted by Lee. I was often the recorder.

"K4823191," she pronounced.

"K4823191," I repeated to ensure accuracy before other data were called. As each bird was done, we held it to drink from sugar water, then opened a hand, and watched freedom retaken. I held my breath as I cradled a tiny, almost weightless jewel and then saw it fluff its iridescence and take off as if nothing had happened.

Sometimes, when Lee handed us a mesh bag he called, "Got one with a band."

"Quick, give me my computer." Work stopped as Susan searched for the number in her old data to find when and where it had been banded. On my first day helping, Lee caught a broad-billed hummingbird that had been banded by them eleven years earlier. It was a long life for a hummingbird after eleven migrations to and from southern Mexico.

Back at the house, I told Linda, "Today we caught one hundred and twenty birds, and half of them were banded."

"Babe, I's so happy you do this, but it takes too long for me. I ain't sitting that long. I walked the kids and met all these cyclists at the Gathering Grounds. Bandit wouldn't go near one a' the bikes and turned out the guy had ridden over a rattler. I told him how Bandit been rattlesnake trained."

We hosted the hummingbird group for meals. On our patio with mountain views, hummingbirds at feeders, and the dogs at our feet, Linda's exuberant clowning made them laugh: *el oso caca in el bosque, adios amoebas.* The interns developed a special affection for the jokester, who in turn was exhilarated by the lively audience. They were our new family, and all of them loved our fur babies—Bailey, Bandit, and Bowtie.

"Look at Bowee's wild wall jumps!" Linda called. "Look at the two of them—they's in love. Even lick each other's orifixes!"

I was devoted to our long-haired tuxedo kitty. "I love you, Bowee," I whispered as I picked him up each morning. When he wanted to go out, he jumped up on the shelf where his leash lay in a wooden bowl. He preferred the big sandbox we had made in the garden enclosure to his indoor litter box, so each day I took him out for an hour.

With Linda off talking to people, I sometimes stayed home. I examined bean seedlings emerging from the damp soil of our garden, tomato leaves disappearing into the

mouths of caterpillars, and grasshoppers hiding among zuc-
chini leaves. For weeks in spring, a mockingbird put on a
variety show at the top of our tall utility pole, making sudden vertical flights and filling the air with songs of thrashers,
house finches, and cardinals. One day, two does and a fawn
made their way close to where I sat. I stood as they ran off,
white tails raised like flags.

I often forgot time as I sat on the wall of the garden bed.
How quickly the years had slipped by. How far I had come
from the career of discovery and the rewarding argument
and camaraderie with Reg, colleagues, and students. I avoided
nostalgic lingering but never stopped feeling fortunate for so
many rich years. The present with Linda was singularly different. Apart from all that was romantic or fun, I had loved
sharing my natural history knowledge and learning about a
person so different from me. She allowed me to discover
more about myself—that I really was rebellious; that despite
my extensive range of life experiences, my good fortune was
no cause for superiority; that I had a passivity allowing me
to accede to all Linda's idiosyncrasies. I had also, curiously,
become the attentive domestic partner despite believing that
women absorbed in assiduously serving their men were bizarre.

LINDA HANKERED AFTER MORE animals. "Babe, let's get
some goats—I love them pygmy goats, and Joan in Sonoita
has babies. I want a pony."

"Ah, bub, and who would look after all these animals?" I
laughed, thinking how her enthusiasm for the chickens and
garden had waned. Driving south of town on a summer day,
we saw a chubby donkey at a ranch near the ghost town of
Harshaw. Linda shouted, "Look!" Stopping the truck, she

raced to the yard and, within minutes, was hugging the donkey over the fence and laughing.

"Look how fat. Must be pregnant. Do you think we could get the foal? Babe, I so want a donkey—a baby donkey."

I was relieved when the rancher later told us the donkey was not pregnant but had a "hay belly."

When one of our chickens got sick, I said, "Let's recycle—the predators can have it."

At nightfall, we settled the ailing chicken on a small roost over a water trough. Next morning, Linda hailed me from the computer, where she was checking the camera cards. "Look at this! Three photos in a row about midnight: chicken on the roost, fox looking at chicken, tail of fox and chicken gone."

We had initially turned one room in my Patagonia house into an office for us both. Linda played poker on her computer while I tried to write. Soon, I would hear, "Oh, you must come and see: there's a boy hooded oriole in the mesquite. Look down there: the medical helicopter's just landed near the clinic. Wonder who they's come for."

When I'd replied "hmm" enough times, she used headphones for music. She eventually moved her computer to the guesthouse, and John extended our Wi-Fi. She could look up the mesquite grassland to oak-covered Red Mountain as she loudly played '60s songs—"I Got You, Babe," "Like a Rolling Stone"—while editing photos. In my office, I could see through an alligator juniper across the valley to Mount Wrightson while Bach or Schubert played in the background. My travels and academic past gave me plenty of material, and I continued writing my entomological memoir, letting myself return to Africa, India, England, and all the curiosity that had thrilled my days.

SOMETIMES SHE CALLED OUT, "I's going to play golf in Nogales."

And I might reply, "Good. I'm off to walk at Temporal Canyon with Bandit."

"See if they's any rockalanches. Love you, bye."

It wasn't that we were growing apart, more that we needed space to ensure we didn't.

In the evenings, we lounged in our outdoor hot tub, surrounded by mesquites, coyotes howling, and unknown animals brushing past in the surrounding bushes. There, we held one another as we looked up at the star-filled sky and watched the rise of the Milky Way in summer, the constant slow transit of satellites, the distant red hovering light of a border patrol helicopter. We were mostly silent. I gave up talking about writing when she said, "When I circumspect, I find it's too reticulating."

We discussed what to plant, which variety of new chickens to get, what Bandit had got up to, how poor Bailey with a mystery illness would sadly have to be euthanized.

LINDA AND I HAD met eight years earlier and for the last three of them were together full time, but she and John were still interdependent. I suspected she had qualms about her "professor doctor doctor." Did she imagine she could fall back on John if I failed her? Or if she tired of me? I understood her insecurities, her fast brain and lack of focus, her childlike qualities, and her lingering entanglement with John. I loved her with all her flaws and foibles, and each time she said, "I loves you, babe," a tender warmth flooded through me.

John's motorbike roared up the driveway on most Saturdays, his Yorkie, Wookie, wearing "doggles." Linda always had jobs. "John, that Pepto-Bismol pink in the guest house makes me puke; you need to paint it."

I didn't know if he needed time with Linda but wondered if he was just waiting for Linda and me to break up. After all, he knew her better than anyone, knew how easily she got bored. But our curious triangle came to feel almost ordinary. We walked the hills with the dogs running free, and I photographed flowers for my compilation of the local flora.

"Come on, Liz, leave them plants," Linda would call as I fell behind to look at a yellow trefoil or the tiniest pink gilia with my Opti visor.

"Just a sec. Saw something different in that wash." And down I went through scrubby sage and red-stemmed Manzanita to photograph a bunch of rosy pussytoes flowers.

On a rough path into the Santa Rita Mountains, Linda's truck rattled over rocks with John at the wheel. I was surprised he automatically drove because Linda insisted on driving when it was just the two of us. Perhaps it was something to do with "I's the guy." I sat in the back and listened to Linda's terse monologue.

"Watch that slope. Go left. That rock too big to drive over." When we saw a group of white-tailed deer, she ordered, "Stop," and we watched them tiptoe through the brush.

ONE WINTER SAW US back in Texas to revisit special places from Linda's youth. John joined us for a week at Goose Island, driving his own car and camping with Wookie in his tent near the motor home. It didn't seem odd to Linda that John was in a tent while we had a big bed in the warm motor home. "He decided to come, so it's what he gets."

John's comment was, "I'll be fine. I got my air bed, sleeping bag, and dog."

Linda and I kept quiet, but in our bed, she whispered, "Set them puppies free. You's got good hooter-monkeys—not like those little dola-mites we saw on that skinny girl today."

The three of us had a simple BBQ Christmas at the campground under the low branches of southern live oaks before walking out on a long pier over shallow brown water, night-herons all along the railings. I have no doubt it evoked memories of past fishing for both Linda and John, but they said little, and it was left to me to make small talk with John. After he returned to Tucson, Linda resumed her more talkative self as we visited other parts of the Gulf coast. Out in the brown water in her waders, a floating container attached to her waist, she cast her rod. My mission was to look after Bandit, watch her catch something, and take the photos.

"This is where we went fishing for red fish. There's the bait shop where the guy always helped with our boat. There's Gaido's restaurant, with the best seafood ever. I loves that gumbo. Could eat crawdads forever." I tagged along, interested in her nostalgic memories, imagining what it was like before she met me, and the years of engagement with John, boats, and fish—the two of them in a tight quarrelsome alliance over thirty-seven years. To me, Linda played down the significance of their friendship, but their past powerful togetherness was manifest in the tone of her comments. They were linked for good.

The best part for me were the whooping cranes at Aransas National Wildlife Refuge. Tall white birds with black faces stepped through reeds or stopped to probe for blue crabs, sapphire claws poking briefly out from a sturdy beak. They were part of a modest flock of cranes bred from a small remaining population in Canada. With Operation Migration, they were taught the migration route from those summer habitats to the Gulf with an ultralight plane as the "parent crane" to guide them.

AFTER FOUR YEARS IN Patagonia, John's visits became less frequent. He explained that he was on a diet, sticking to his protein drinks while Linda and I ate spaghetti.

"Well, you's overweight, so it's a good thing," Linda observed.

Some weeks later, he wore new shorts and an ironed cotton shirt.

"Something's up," Linda noted after he had gone.

After a few more visits, he told us, "Yeah, I joined Match. com."

I was pleased for him, but Linda's feelings were ambiguous. She had taken him literally when he said he would never leave her. And despite everything, she still needed security or support from him. Part of her life had been telling him what to do. And he needed to be told as much as she needed to give orders. But there had been mutiny.

"He wanted that motorsickle, but I couldn't bear him riding one. I seen so many deaths on them. So I told him he can't ever have one, but then he got one anyway. I was furious, and I can't drive behind him cos I don't want to see him killed in front a' me."

Match.com produced a divorced woman as Linda chafed with the uncertainties. "Deb's gotta be a girlie one that just wants sex and money."

John was reassuring. "It's not serious, Lin, and I don't want a separation. Deb just said she wanted a relationship with a married man."

I WOULDN'T BE DRAWN into discussion of John's actions. I saw both sides, and she saw only one. Some months later, he suggested a legal separation, which led to an argument. Linda asserted, "We's getting a divorce." It was ugly and distressing for months on end. The two of them had been interdependent for so long, it was inevitably a bitter period. Linda's teasing and anecdotes petered out.

John brought her boxes to Patagonia—the memorabilia, all her adoptive parents' special papers like school reports and other childhood mementos her mother had kept, and her father's wartime records. There were photography awards, textbooks illustrated with her photos, and the few possessions of value. Then the man who had been Linda's sole companion and friend since she was fourteen was gone for good.

Her energy declined, and tears flowed. "Paul gone, John gone, no relatives. Losing Paul and then the divorce been the real emotional stresses of my life, much worse than the deaths of Mom and Dad, though I loved them the most."

I tried to put myself in her place and get her to think of other interests.

"Want to come to the post office?"

"No energy, babe. Can't even walk up the hill."

"Well, let's see what the chickens have given us."

"You get the eggs. Do your flower thing. Whatever."

Now I was the only partner, and we would be together for as long as it might last. If it did last. I did have hopes, though I never gave a thought to the distant future. I was ever aware that Linda's enthusiasms could be short-lived, so I had adjusted to living simply in the present. Somehow, though, we had to try to rise out of the present gloom. I believed Linda's wretchedness would pass, but as time went by, nothing changed. "I don't wanna be anywhere that reminds me of John," she said tearfully one morning. Sweet, old-fashioned Patagonia and all our projects lost their appeal as she spent days watching sitcoms or house-restoration shows.

She became good at stock market trading, but she was also looking at house listings in Tucson. I had to do something. My first idea was to book another trip to Australia, but I had wanted the idyllic years in this dream home to last the rest of my life. Now I needed to prime myself for change once again, and I mentally worked to accept Patagonia's limitations. Essential trips to Tucson had become arduous, friends had left or died, mining projects threatened its serenity. On top of that, I was now doing all the work. Clearly, my love of the little Patagonia paradise was not enough for us both.

There would be that trip to Australia, but meanwhile, I continued despondently with my plant survey and worked with a new group in Patagonia, Borderland Restoration. Retired ecologist Ron Pulliam had started the project, replanting overgrazed regions with native plants and building gabions made of stones across barren washes to allow rainwater to soak in and improve plant regrowth. He could have been one of the local ranchers, with his long, lank hair, deeply lined face, and overalls covering a big paunch. He welcomed all comers who were willing to add something.

In the mountains, I wandered with Bandit, gradually coming to terms with the inevitable. It was Patagonia or Linda. I thought back to the drab bedsit of my first year in London or the grubby little apartment in steamy Ibadan up seven flights of sticky stairs and later the Julia Morgan redwood house in Berkeley with a view of the Golden Gate Bridge. Every place had been engaging in its own way, and no place had everything. I contemplated the current crossroads. Patagonia had captivated me, but Tucson had other benefits like the music and university friends. Eventually, I examined listings of Tucson houses myself.

"I think I have found a house, bub," I said, showing Linda the website.

"Fuck, babe, that's the one I's got!" And I welcomed the return of smiles.

Two such different people, with such different tastes in almost everything, had picked the same house. Given the coincidence, I needed to act quickly. When would we ever agree on another place? But we were due to fly to Australia three days later.

"It will probably still be there when we get back," Linda said half-heartedly.

I looked at her. "No, we better go and look."

We rushed up to the city. There was nowhere to put the motor home and very little garden, but somehow it had the right feel. We wandered through the area, and Linda connected with people who would become neighbors. I could sense her spirit rising.

"I love it here, babe. They's all so nice. And the house is solar and everything."

"Yes, bub, I like it, and we can walk to concerts and restaurants downtown."

"And you can see all your professor people on campus. I want you to have your science friends and writers and symphony."

I put my arm around her as she kissed me on the cheek with tears in her eyes.

We made an offer, flew off to Australia, and carried out the negotiations across the Pacific. When we got back to Arizona, we owned a house in Armory Park by downtown Tucson, the Patagonia house was for sale, and the motor home was hooked up in a Patagonia RV park, where I could stay

on visits. The sound of "I so excited, babe" told me we had
made the right decision and helped me feel resilient. It had
all happened suddenly, but I could manage a new adventure.
My whole life had been a succession of them, and now, with
Linda, we had done something new—we made a big choice
together.

17 A New Life

IT WAS SPRING WHEN we left the mesquite grassland in the mountains. Palo verde trees in Tucson covered with welcoming yellow blossoms took me back to Reg's last yellow April days. But gratitude for my past had replaced mourning, and I needed to address the clutter of junk still left in Patagonia.

"You go deal with the mess," Linda snapped.

"What will I do with your big drawers of mats and frames?"

"I don't give a damn."

I stood looking down at her as she lolled in a chair, arms hanging. "Do you want to break up? Separate?" I didn't know what was wrong with her.

She began sobbing, and I said no more.

Alone in Patagonia, I packed up all Linda's treasures and sold the big map drawers where she had kept framing mats. I gave away furniture, bags of garden tools, chickens and chicken food, trail cameras and troughs as I thought of Linda, miserable in Tucson, and wondered. All her found items in the mesquite trees were left hanging—unidentified rusty objects, vintage food cans and lids from old boxes of blasting caps from mining days. I looked at the vintage metal press and remembered how excited she was to have come across such a prize.

It was a sad and lonely task. For eleven years, the last six in Patagonia, we'd had such fun, so much travel, and constant discoveries about each other, and now she sat listless and irascible in her chair. There had been other undercurrents that came to me as I worked. Linda had a control issue and had called the shots over many unimportant details of our lives. But we had lived in my house with my belongings, my taste in décor and art. I had been the house manager and boss. The imbalance hadn't struck me before.

When, at twenty-two, I left home to travel the world, I felt I had left behind our family conceits and the feelings of superiority I had grown up with, and in the intervening years, I had looked back on my much-loved mother's pretentions with a mixture of disdain and amusement. The echoes of her directives and her assurances of our esteemed class had been dismissed in my daily life. Yet I had kept a thread of that superiority—surreptitious, seductive, secret—a remnant of those childhood teachings.

Back in Tucson, in the house we had bought together, I determined we would find balance.

Linda always looked after the vehicles and loved everything to do with them. Her eyes swept the big garage.

"I want to be in charge of all this space and paint it lime green."

"Of course," I said, taking her hand.

Within days, she was at the paint store, but she didn't last long at the work. She whimpered, "I's got no energy, babe." We had Jesse, a painter friend from Patagonia, turn the dirty white into lush lime.

Inside, we surveyed the endless white. I turned to Linda.

"You will be in the TV room more than me. You pick the color."

Linda took out her laptop and looked at colors. "Royal blue, lime-green ceiling, red trim."

I tried to imagine that mix. "And your office?"

Her sober choice surprised me. "A black chalk wall for drawing on, the rest gray. I know you's going to have boring stuff."

I chose yellow for my office. Then we had Juli from Prickly Pear Painting help us choose for other rooms. I explained, "It's hard when we're such opposites."

Juli turned each color card toward us. If either of us said no, it went in one pile; if both of us said okay, it went in another. The okay pile was small, but Juli mixed the resulting blues and beiges on different walls, and we were satisfied.

As Juli prepped the dining room, she looked at the table. "I love that. It's fifties Scandinavian, and if you ever want to sell, count me in."

Linda was fascinated as she focused on the table. I told her Reg and I had bought it in London. "We gotta get stuff to go with it. I seen a place on Broadway called Ralph's Fifties Furniture."

It was there that we found a matching settee.

Linda hung some of her best street photography on several walls. "Them two old women's my favorite. I call it 'London hookers.'" Two rooms were for her nature pictures, and we hung monster caterpillars in the master bathroom. A big oil painting of the Whetstone mountains by James Cook found a home on a dark-blue feature wall facing the front door, and all the paintings of trees went to the master bedroom. Linda chose the brilliant lime-green color for the outside of the house, and I picked the pollinator plants to enhance the small outdoor space.

Linda's fatigue, irritability, and depression were explained when we learned she had Graves' disease with various complications. But new drugs helped, and she grew back some of her energy. She was excited about fixing the house. "Babe, we gotta have some decent lights."

"Oh my god, look at that," Linda shouted at the lighting store. She pointed to a long metal wave chandelier with dozens of small LED lights along the curved nickel bars. I would never have chosen it but found myself admiring it.

I looked across a gap in the mass of light fixtures. "I want the chrome spider thing for the living room."

"Oh, yeah, babe, love it."

Going home, we passed the Tucson Hot Tub store, and I turned to her. "Bub, we've got to come back here when you've rested, eh? I know you're dying for a hot tub."

We chose the smallest for a tiny patio and a few days later, watched it dangling from a crane as it was lowered into place. On the wall above she hung her prize photo of a raven's head printed on a sheet of aluminum as big as the tub. Visitors to the house looking through the glass door to the patio invariably commented, "What an amazing photograph."

Meanwhile, we enjoyed all the benefits of living downtown in a bicultural city. "We's in Tucson, babe; we gotta go do stuff. Ernesto next door said it's Second Saturday Night with bands and food trucks and break dancing and them Scottish people dancing in kilts with bagpipes."

During Cyclovia, when streets were closed to traffic, I joined the families riding bicycles, stopped at stalls to look at all things bicycle, and listened to mariachi bands. I raced past individuals playing accordions, guitars, and flutes on my vintage red bike, a gift from my students during Berkeley days.

Linda chose shows—*Mamma Mia, Phantom of the Opera, Chicago.*

Despite my sadness at leaving Patagonia, I did enjoy the entertainments, seminars, readings, and contact with friends at the university. On her good days, Linda and I walked the neighborhood with Bandit, and she talked to everyone. In laidback, carefree Patagonia, she had enjoyed the people, but she found more common ground with the academics, environmentalists, writers, and artists in Armory Park. An only child often prefers the company of adults, and she had been one of those, but I felt her super-fast brain was the significant factor in making connection with the mental energy of many new neighbors. The one-mile walk could take a couple of hours. "So many cool people. A ton a' PhDs. You gotta correlate and postulate and come up with the right prescription."

Linda loved to repeat what she had heard on her own walks. "Them new people on Laos Street moved from Oregon; got a pit bull, but they's liberal. The lady down at the corner works at Raytheon. I wonder if she knows John."

I said, "Jill cast aspersions on that new neighbor, Lee."

"Yeah, she full of asparagus."

The first years when the idea of being together 24/7 was scary or even shocking had slowly and inexorably yielded to a comfortable life of togetherness. My life before Linda, up until Reg's death, had been so rewarding and full, I was satisfied to let Linda make decisions and ready to commit to whatever followed. It had a lot to do with a passive streak I retained, which was one of my father's traits. How, otherwise, would Mother have been so painfully taken by surprise when the bailiff came to tell us we had to get out of our house? His difficulty managing money had never been known, let alone discussed. He never demonstrated anxiety.

I WANTED TO SHOW Linda San Francisco and Berkeley—home when I was a professor at the University of California. Now the flight enthusiast, she was eager. "We gotta go Southwest; they's the best, and we gotta be sure to check in at exactly twenty-four hours before takeoff to get the best choice of seats."

Together we selected the Kensington Park Hotel near Nob Hill. Built in 1925, it was a slightly old-fashioned, gothic-style building, central in the city of steep hills. Walking to the great red span of the Golden Gate Bridge made Linda gasp. "Just like on TV. We going to Fisherman's Wharf?"

"Of course," and there we ate fish on the wharf and watched street entertainers like Bush Man. He hid, holding a dense tree branch in front of him, until a group of people neared. Then he leapt out to scare them. They always jumped up in surprise and then laughed at the moment's absurdity. It was such a simple joke, yet we found it killingly funny.

In Golden Gate Park, we sauntered by lakes and meadows to the Japanese Tea Garden. We met an old friend and former postdoc from my Berkeley days at the newly rebuilt California Academy of Sciences museum, and the three of us roamed through the aquarium. Linda went ahead observing fish while I reminisced about past times with my friend. "Remember old Hal? Did no research but asked piercing questions at seminars like the one at your job seminar." I returned with, "Reg and I loved the dinner parties with you students and postdocs much more than anything with the faculty."

Especially fun was showing Linda the Berkeley campus. "Look, bub, there's the building with the entomology department and insect museum." I pointed to a classical revival building with a circular front. "It's called Wellman Hall, and it's over one hundred years old."

She looked it over in wonder. "Your place, eh, babe?"

"Yes, that's where I taught classes and battled with the department chair."

"You sad not being here?"

"Not really, though it was a great time. I wouldn't have met you here."

We walked around to the courtyard at the back of the building. I used to look down to the pollarded planes in two rows, their knobby fists signaling upward on winter mornings and their leafy heads shivering in summer breezes. As I peered out at them, I marveled at the strange fate of being a professor there. In London, when Reg had said there was a job in Berkeley that described me, I was aghast at the idea of going to the United States, but I did apply for it, and when I got the job, it was intensely thrilling. How quickly I learned about individualism! Looking after number one first was not something I had needed to do in Australia or England.

As we walked on, I explained, "This is Sproul Plaza, where a man in a polka-dot suit used to lie down with legs in the air, and Orange Man would stand by and watch."

"What's Orange Man?"

"Well, I was told he never recovered from drugs. I used to see him walking around Berkeley hanging paper oranges in all the trees."

"You percolating in my head," she said as she held my hand.

BACK IN TUCSON, LINDA took stock of the vehicles. The big motor home in Patagonia that served as my retreat had been a problem with fixes that never lasted, so she spent hours fighting the makers until they finally agreed to buy it back, replacing it with a quality campervan. Her beloved old Toyota truck was too heavy for the campervan to tow.

"I gotta sell it anyways—just another thing reminding me of John."

She chose a Jeep. At the dealership, she looked at me. "You ain't driving it." But I had no desire to touch her special car. She took me on memorable four-wheel drives like the back road up the Santa Catalina Mountains that loom over Tucson. Alone on the rocky road, Linda crawled over boulders and across trenches as I stared at the lonely hills and valleys with their patches of yellow from *Tecoma* flowers and deep washes highlighted by the light greens of cottonwood trees.

"Great, eh, babe?"

On days when Linda had no energy, "You do your stuff, babe. I's watching TV."

At those times, I joined old friends for the symphony, opera, or a poetry reading.

WE HAD GOOD VISITS to New Zealand and Canada, but trips in the new campervan worked better because we could take off at short notice and stop whenever Linda needed to rest. I went with her when she met up with the Milky Way tracers to photograph the starry night as the Milky Way rose above the southern horizon. Linda became friends with June in the flashlight darkness, and she showed Linda a headless white mannequin she had used for a different photography project. It ended up on our front porch, and Linda called it Nigel.

I was hooked on stars. We camped for a few days in the Superstition Mountains, east of Phoenix, with their rugged peaks, canyons, and lakes, and walked in the evenings to viewpoints to watch the Milky Way rise over the mountains.

"Can't see it, bub," I said.

But Linda had the position worked out, and gradually my

eyes accommodated enough to make out the faint shimmering masses. With Linda preoccupied shooting photos, I gazed at the immensity, the distance that couldn't be imagined, and my thoughts turned to the shortness of our lives on this small planet. Through my life, I had been obsessed with mortality and in the dark years found it comforting to know that life would end. I even found comfort in the possibility of suicide, though I never came very close. Yet the strangeness of the idea that all my thinking and emotions evaporated at death made me love every flower and sunset more. Watching the stars, I silently confronted twin emotions—the appreciation of life and the solace of death.

At home, Linda edited her photos.

"Look, babe."

"Gorgeous, bub. But the stars weren't so bright really."

"You just gotta enhance the contrast in Photoshop, babe. Is that cool or what?"

ON THE NEXT BIG summer camping trip, we headed for New Mexico and Colorado. It was freeing to be on the road again, forgetting the increasingly acrimonious national politics. Linda drove as usual with '60s music playing, and there were people to chat with wherever we stopped to camp. And there were the cars to admire, of course.

"Hey, a 1958 Corvette! There goes a 1962 Thunderbird. Oh my god, look at the tailfin on the '58 Chevy Impala!"

I smiled. Her excitement about cars was still a mystery to me, but I loved her engagement.

IN COLORADO, WE MADE it to Crested Butte and visited my friends and former colleagues working at the Rocky Mountain Biological Laboratory, way up at almost ten thousand feet. Reg and I had been to this alpine paradise years earlier to work with my student Dave, whose project was to determine how blue lycaenid butterflies chose among different kinds of lupines on which to lay eggs. One of the butterfly species was a specialist, which is always an advantage. Its larvae fed on leaves of one kind of lupine, so food was available for the whole season. The other species had to be more of a generalist because it fed only on flowers. Each kind of lupine had different short flowering times, so this butterfly needed to utilize whichever lupine was available during its flight time.

Linda stayed at the campground while my friend Nancy took me on a walk in the flower-filled mountains, and we bent over to look in detail at mauve columbines, pink queen's crown, blue lupines, bluebells, and penstemons. I pondered the magnanimous multicolored slopes topped by rocky peaks as I saw ahead of me a slim woman with natural poise, shoulder-length hair, and soft voice. I admired her work on evolution but loved her for who she was—caring and understated.

She turned. "You didn't bring Linda on the walk?"

"She doesn't have the vigor. She is with Bandit at the stream by the campground."

Nancy was the friend who most understood Linda. Brought up in a big Catholic family with so many different characters, including one severely autistic brother, she had an appreciation of people who were a bit out of the ordinary, people who were not academics.

Back at the campground, Howard, Nancy's husband and colleague, joined us. His dark eyes sparkled as he laughed, his fast brain more than matching Linda's as they each shot out jokes in a kind of competition (though Linda often forgot the punch line). Nancy and I smiled. We both had plenty of ideas, but we were slower thinkers. Each of us had a partner whose thoughts sometimes came faster than the words to express them.

That evening, I thought about my attraction to plants and how I loved to examine them, name them, study how they grew, and find out who ate them. Then I realized it was the same with insects; I had been caught up all my life in the enjoyment of how the different species functioned and evolved. My earliest memories include finding out the names of all the butterflies and beetles in my mother's garden. In some ways, it was not so different from Linda's passion for cars. Each of us had learned the language of what engaged us: plants and insects and their biology versus cars and trucks and their mechanics.

As Linda and I took our campervan all over the western states, we felt a commonality that enhanced the new parity in our lives. We were reaching the point of realizing we really were together in some permanent way.

In Patagonia, I had worked on my book manuscript, *Six Legs Walking*, a memoir of my entomological life with Reg. In Tucson, the book was accepted for publication, and later, Linda came with me to many of my readings. Whenever I showed her a good review, she said, "You's the real writer, eh, babe? I loves my writer."

Meanwhile, I began a new writing project. Linda was thrilled that the new book was to be about us. "What did you write today?"

"Oh, I revised some bits and added a few anecdotes."

"Okay, you put in some antidotes. What else?"

I gave her chapters to read at an early stage to make sure the words I gave her were accurate, and she corrected a few of them. But if she was feeling good, my absorption in writing sometimes became tedious. "You just writing for your bemusement."

Even after thirteen years together, communication with Linda could still be complicated. She was often frustrated with my being somewhere else in my head when she talked. But she habitually jumped from one topic to another so that it was also hard to know exactly what she was referring to. Often it didn't matter because her thoughts had moved on before I had a chance to respond. Once we were chatting about the campervan when Linda said, "Yeah, I think we might've had Steve visit."

"Who are you talking about?"

"Our neighbor Momi's outdoor cat. He's called Steve." Another case of her corkscrew train of thought.

She loved to laugh at me. My lack of dance rhythm, the words I used. Walking together along a path after rain, we came across a squashed slug.

"Completely eviscerated," I remarked, bending down to look.

"Yeah, all evaporated." She laughed.

But I knew that such comments were reason to relax and know she was feeling good. The good days were a blessing. When sentences were hard to figure out, I complained, "I don't know what you are saying."

"You ain't listening, or you's deaf," she would shout and then try again.

"That's not what you said before," I would reply.

My reserve played into her control issue, making it easy for her to be bossy, but rows were few. I had already lightened up about Linda's inability to think beyond the next day. Well, it doesn't really matter if we have no plans at all. I didn't want to watch TV while we ate, but I ended up accepting that it would be our habit. I was the one to finish the jobs Linda started with such aplomb. I would put the tools away.

The constant laughter of our early years moderated, but

it remained an important part of our relationship. During housework, Linda often stopped to joke and dance.

"Give me a hug."

"What about a kiss?"

"What about titties?"

"Sure, I will get the kitties."

We both loved Bandit. How he jumped joyfully when he took the little yoghurt cups he had licked clean to the recycling box. As he slowed down, we wondered how long we had left with him, and then we found a kitten. Walking close to a nearby warehouse, the meowing gray-and-white kitty emerged from tall grass, approaching Linda. "He wants love more than food. Look at that."

He became our adored Monkey, with hundreds of photos on social media. Our affection for our three fur babies became a reason not to travel at all, though I was sometimes restless. "Bub, we need to plan, or we don't go anywhere."

"But I's never sure I's going to feel good ahead of time."

Linda's photography passions changed over time—street people, cars, Milky Way, storm chasing, pet portraits, infrared. She was energized by online programs on photography and astronomy, and I came to love Tucson more as I rode around on my bike, relentlessly photographing historical, artistic, botanical, or weird items around town. Since our first bizarre meeting, many windows had been opened for each of us in the Tucson desert, in the Patagonia Mountains, and downtown. We had also learned from each other. There was always something novel to learn and enjoy. There were constant new vistas in my life that kept me tuned in to world. I agreed with Albert Einstein, who said, "Life is like riding a bicycle. To keep your balance, you must keep moving."

With all that we had experienced together, Linda and I had finally realized equality and equanimity. Friends sometimes seemed surprised at how well we seemed to manage with our vastly different personalities, and I wondered if being older had helped; the idealism of youth and the search for perfection had not been a motivation for us. More mellow, we both wanted to be flexible and adaptable, and the feeling of an enduring relationship had descended on us. In 2015, the Supreme Court had legalized gay marriage, but did we want it? Neither of us ever mentioned marriage. I didn't think about the future at all, any more than I thought about how much time was left to us, but I did keep a readiness for the unexpected.

18 The Last Bridge

AMONG MY EARLIEST MEMORIES is a garden at my Sydney kindergarten where the teacher unsuccessfully implored me to join ring-a-ring o' roses games on the lawn. Years later, Mother told me the teacher had pronounced me asocial. It was the beginning of a lifelong predilection for independence and solitude. As soon as I was allowed, there were the many solitary bushwalks and whole days rowing my dinghy on the Brisbane River.

After sailing away from Australia at twenty-two and indulging bohemian needs, I stood one foggy morning on Westminster Bridge in London, a city I knew so thrillingly from books. Alone above the muddy tide of the Thames, the intensity of independence and anonymity surged through me—an electric current of excitement.

Within a few years in England, I became an entomologist and fell for my professor, Reg. We shared a passionate curiosity in our research. We puzzled over how grasshopper taste buds detected plant wax or determined how they knew what and how much to eat. I cherished his unusual appearance—a flat face with a mole on one cheek. I loved his teasing Cockney phrases like "use your loaf" when I couldn't figure something out and his engagement with nonsense as we read Edward Lear or his clownish imitation of elephants or pigeons. As with Linda later, we shared a love of nonsense and lack of interest in religion. At the time, he was different from anyone I had ever met, but our interests were perfectly harmonized, and he made me feel I was so much more than I believed myself to be. We became lovers, soulmates totally absorbed with each other, though unmarried for many years. That was an act of rebelliousness at the time, though fitting for the Swinging Sixties in London.

"How about getting married, Lizzie?" he would say at intervals.

But I didn't need a piece of paper. It didn't matter to me that some folks disapproved. Or that during a job interview at Oxford University, the vice chancellor, who happened to be a friend, told me that not being married to Reg would probably count against me. I didn't get the job.

But in 1983, I had an offer of a professorship in Berkeley. Reg gave up his career for me to go, but without a job, marriage was required for his immigration to the United States. We chose the Chelsea registry office for a nonreligious ceremony, not realizing it was the hip place for civil unions. The office was inside Chelsea Old Town Hall in the Royal Borough of Kensington and Chelsea; built in Victorian times in neoclassical style, it had plain rooms of different sizes. We had just two witnesses, so our wedding took place in a flower-filled room with just six oak chairs and a table. It felt calm and peaceful. We had to wait, though, as the wedding was delayed by twenty minutes. An English girl was marrying an Iranian man, and the government had made a provision for an official to privately talk to the girl in such cases to warn her that her beau may have one or more wives in Iran.

I was happy for the delay as I contemplated the meaning of marriage and ruminated on how much of life was determined not by choice but by events—without the enticing job offer in California, we would probably have stayed in England and never married. I knew that twelve thousand miles away, my mother would not have approved of "living in sin" or marrying a man whose father was an independent builder. But nothing would interfere with my chosen path and need to be myself.

As usual in civil weddings then, we had our set pieces. In my turn, "I declare that I know of no legal reason why I, Elizabeth Bernays, may not be joined in marriage to Reginald Chapman. I call upon these persons, here present, to witness that I do take thee to be my lawful wedded husband." The registrar finished with, "Reginald and Elizabeth, you have both made the declarations prescribed by law and have made a solemn and binding contract with each other in the presence of witnesses here assembled. It therefore gives me the greatest honor and privilege to announce that you are now husband and wife together."

It all seemed solemn, and I felt surprisingly fulfilled. I thought how curious for a wedding ceremony to have an impact when I had never taken the conventional path. How odd it felt to have done such an orthodox thing. Even in my research, I had advanced by taking rebellious new directions, paths that disregarded fashionable theories. My thoughts were interrupted when Reg said, "What about a celebration lunch?"

Our two witnesses were friend and colleague Wally and Reg's daughter, Anne, from a previous marriage. We were a very close foursome. We were in a taxi before discovering that Reg had already reserved a table at L'Escargot in Soho, then rated the best, and oldest, French restaurant in London. We stepped into the famous old Georgian townhouse with a snail painting on a projecting notice above the door.

The black-suited maître d'hôtel welcomed us. "You will probably enjoy the salon bleu."

There were several elaborately set tables. Seated at ours, we joked about which remarkable dish to choose. Not escargots with wild champignons, not baked homard with garlic butter, not tournedos Rossini. Eventually, after tasting our glasses of sauvignon blanc, Wally went for salmon, Anne for gigot d'agneau. Reg and I shared a chateaubriand that was so tender it literally fell off our forks. Leisurely, we drank two (or was it three?) bottles of 1978 Chateau Neuf du Pape. I know that we all laughed a lot, but apart from the gaiety and Reg's twinkling eyes, I remember little. We went home by bus, and nothing really felt different.

The next day we were busy with a new set of observations on the activity of locusts. We found that individuals had a fifteen-minute rhythm so that one could predict when they were likely to walk about or feed.

ON A COOL SPRING morning thirty years later, I rested under the big mesquite tree on my patio in Tucson, staring with nostalgia at the scene Reg and I had so cherished. In the terrible vacancy of his death, I had filled the days and nights racing to finish our research projects and write the papers, as if time itself were ending. But then came exhaustion. I absently watched quail with chicks in tow scratching among the fallen yellow flowers, and I focused on the long coos of mourning doves. The name seemed right for them, and the sound reflected my melancholy.

How often we had watched the desert wildlife from under these feathery branches! During his last week, with labored breathing, he had whispered, "Lizzie, I need my bed out here." I looked down at the man I had loved for thirty-seven years. I bent and kissed him on the top of his head. Then I dragged a bed out through the Arizona room and into the dappled shade, where he could sleep with the mesquite flowers falling onto him and wake to hear the springtime cardinal's song.

During the last years of Reg's terminal illness, hugging had been as far as intimacy went. After his death, I needed solitude to reflect on our great love affair, but over time, long-forgotten sexual desire swelled. I was surprised. Libido rose whenever I wept for what was lost. Friends who noticed my red eyes and thin face advised me to find a support group, an idea that was anathema to me. Weeks passed, and desire became lesbian desire. I thought about all the older women who turn to lesbian relationships as widows, but I had been attracted to women before. There had been tall, imposing Sandy, a lesbian who quite bewitched me, but in my charmed life with Reg, I never let such a thing surface. It wasn't until a year after he died that the desire became compelling.

Eventually, I did the unthinkable—I found a support group, run by Wingspan. Across the circle was Texan Linda. I only understood parts of what was a totally new dialect, but I was enraptured by something so novel and the pleasure of being controversial in "switching teams." We slowly emerged from the strangeness of our disparities to embrace a half-time affair. I looked beyond the social prejudices of my upbringing and a rich academic life. Linda looked beyond her lack of education and life with John, her only companion since childhood. Over eight years, we slowly become engaged in a serious full-time relationship. Fourteen years went by. We had learned to share our contrasted lives, and permanence was in the air, but I was reluctant to think about any formal bond. I didn't need another marriage. Yet I knew my desire for autonomy was not shared by her. She gave no clear hint, but I was sure she would welcome marriage. I thought about Linda's general insecurity and her fascination with legitimizing documents; how she was thrilled with all my academic ones, the ones she didn't share. As with Reg, though for a different reason, it was Linda who needed that piece of paper. She was the lover who could hardly believe she had been chosen. A document mattered.

One day, I woke her early and took her by the shoulders. "Wakey wakey."

She opened her eyes with a frown. "What happened?"

Smiling, I stroked her longer, now-gray hair that was every which way and looked into her dark, still-sleepy eyes. "Let's get married."

"Really?" She jumped out of bed with the wide smile that had so charmed me from the start. "Married! Oh, yes, babe," she said before a big hug. Then she twirled me around the bedroom singing "All the Single Ladies."

"We gotta have the *biggest* party ever and a *ton* of amusement."

These needs didn't speak to me, but her enthusiasm and excitement made me happy. *Why not just have fun and let go of the past? Let my sweetheart do all that she wants for the party.* And I knew it would have to be a splash to celebrate this crazy partnership. I wrote to my cousin Cherry in Australia: "You'll have to come over—this will be my last hurrah!"

Linda found the Whistle Stop Depot for our October wedding—an old warehouse with recycled materials decorating the building and garden.

"Liz, you send out keep-the-date emails. You can do the words better'n me, but don't put what it's for."

We had many friends, and I had relatives from Australia and England. Also included were all kinds of people talkative Linda had befriended here and there in the street or doing jobs on the house, plus the family from the RV repairers and the guy who fixed the windshield. I thought, *Oh well, why not?*, and I later ended up sending out two hundred invitations. Linda made whimsical cards with her own photo of chimpanzees from Sydney Zoo, and instructions to wear crazy costumes to the party, where there would be an open bar, informal dining, music, and dancing.

Apart from a piece of paper, the charm of a big party was a winner for Linda. She chose the photographers, the music, and the entertainments. It fell to me to organize details to ensure against chaos.

"Make spreadsheets," Linda ordered.

I walked to the mailbox.

"No looking at replies until you get home," Linda warned.

Most people had checked *enthusiastically accept*; a few had checked *regretfully declined*. A few checked these as well as the joke options: *enthusiastically decline* and *regretfully accept*.

In the feverish excitement, we suddenly realized we had to think about the actual ceremony. A friend suggested Patrick, a large, bearded chaplain with a big smile who was a regular Tucson Santa Claus at Christmas.

"We's atheists, so we don't want any God shit," Linda declared when he came to visit.

"That's alright." He laughed. "I'm more of an agnostic these days."

We all agreed that humor and simplicity should rule. There would be no procession, no big entrance, no poetry or literary reading, and no serious homily.

Walking to the town hall to get a marriage license, I joked, "Why are we getting married?"

"So I won't have to pee on you to mark my territory!"

Our marriage would be a final fulfillment of the lesbian yearning Linda had lived through all her life. For me, it was a delight to give her this moment. I thought about my very low-key marriage to Reg and the frenzy of my coming marriage to Linda. I had not elected for either, but in both cases, any thoughts of personal freedom faded into insignificance.

There was so much to laugh about with Linda, with her excitement over every detail, including her finding a place fittingly called Loudmouth to make our wedding outfits. But when it was just two days away, Linda fell in the street and hurt herself. So I ran all the errands, greeted guests who had flown in and partied with them, and constantly checked details. And then it was the day.

AFTER THE HOUR OF greetings, the children's mariachi band played from the ramp of the Whistle Stop as nearly two hundred costumed guests took their seats in the garden below. Dozens of cell phones were raised, and a host of parents stood on the side and joined the cheering audience. The clapping had hardly stopped when Black Cat, Ajia in drag and normally our hairdresser, made a grand entrance down the steps. Extravagant, multicolored robes flowed to his ankles. He was more than six feet tall, very black, and very beautiful with a dark, wavy wig and a wide white smile. He lip-synced the songs, and clapping guests sang along to Beyoncé's song about "putting a ring on it."

As the opening theme song from *2001: A Space Odyssey* began, I wheeled Linda in her Loudmouth parti-colored pants to the front and faced the crowd in my Hello Kitty outfit.

"Welcome, everyone. With puppy love, we are gathered here as we celebrate the tie between two people who see each other as the cat's meow. Linda says love is knowing that when she texts me, I will reply. I say love is when she lets me read without her talking."

Three videographers dressed as mermaids drew close. One of them was muralist Joe Pagac, complete with coconut knockers. Photographer Christopher, with afro wig in rainbow colors and face painted for Day of the Dead, squatted in front.

Patrick, wearing vestments and Santa Claus hat, began, "We are gathered to witness and celebrate the marriage of Liz and Linda. We come together not to mark the start of a relationship but to acknowledge and strengthen a bond that already exists."

Linda interrupted with a grin and looked at me. "Your eyes are like turds floating in a cesspool."

Patrick played along, laughing as Linda leaned toward him on crutches, held up her phone to get selfies, and imitated our kitty, Bowtie, cleaning his face.

The Rosenthal family sat in the front row dressed as the life cycle of the monarch butterfly: egg, caterpillar, pupa, and butterfly. How like my inventive friend Martha to get the family dressed for the entomologist. I smiled as I saw my cousin Cherry in a sari talking to my great-niece, Sophie, wearing a dirndl.

"Do you, Liz and Linda, pledge to build a life of mutual respect, compassion, generosity, and patience toward each other?"

"We do."

"Do you pledge to recognize each other's individuality and celebrate each other's uniqueness as a strength in marriage while at the same time guard one another's weaknesses with understanding, support, and inspiration?"

"We do."

"And do you pledge to share the love you have for each other with all living beings?"

"We do."

We called for Bandit, our Labrador, and he came running, a GoPro camera on his back together with a cowboy doll in a saddle. Bandit carried the cheap stainless-steel rings we had worn for years on our right hands, and I removed them from the little pocket on his collar.

"With these rings, I marry you," Patrick said as we put the rings on each another, and he finished, "I now pronounce you puppy and kitten."

The crowd cheered boisterously, and the bar became a huddle of costumes. Two men in pink tutus pranced up and down the equipment ramp, and a couple dressed as policemen played a game of chase with two kids in prisoner garb.

As we ate our Mexican feast at multicolored tables, Darth Vader approached Linda and laughed. "Hello, Stephen Hawking. Get up outta that wheelchair!"

When the crowd began to disperse, Wonder Woman wheeled Linda around some of the tables, and Andy Warhol with various masked figures waved goodbye. Finally, a big brown bear drove us home.

It took days to fully realize that yes, we were married, wife and wife, spouses! From her wheelchair, Linda would introduce me: "This is my wife" and then laugh loudly at the strangeness. For Linda, there was a cloud of happiness, despite having broken her femur and needing months to recover. She had the best wedding photo printed for the desk in my office. Linda rising from her wheelchair on crutches, Patrick in his Santa Claus hat, and Bandit at our feet. It was a reminder of how far we had come from when I was intensely aware of our obvious incompatibilities and anticipated no more than an exciting, short-lived affair.

Over the fourteen years, Linda's world, so weirdly unfamiliar to me, unfolded as mine became less strange to her. Underneath the massive layers of contrasting life experiences, we found similarities. We were both rebels with little care as to what others thought of us. We loved our fur family. We were addicted to fun. Our enchantment with the living world overrode concern with anything preternatural.

IN THE QUIET OF my office, I reflect on the colorful merriment and effervescence of our party and the bridges crossed; how it cements the affection that grew from our original fascination. Reg and I had had the easy and instinctive togetherness of soulmates, and despite some similarities between Reg and Linda, and a rebellious element surrounding each relationship, Linda and I learned to embrace something elemental about our common humanity and commitment across a vast divide.

I turn to the window that looks out through a *Tecoma* tree to a quiet street beyond. I watch big, shiny, black carpenter bees at the yellow bellflowers. One of them chews a hole at the base of a flower and steals the nectar without collecting pollen. A male Gila woodpecker squawks as it drinks sugar water from the hummingbird feeder and chases off a female. The tamale man pushes his cart along the street, and a tall girl with gray dreadlocks rides by on her bike with an Australian shepherd puppy running beside her. Down the alley, a ginger cat looks up at a sweet acacia tree, where the gentle voice of a mourning dove floats out into the warm dry air.

Linda and Liz

Made in the USA
Las Vegas, NV
11 March 2024

87022708R00143